Praise for *Our Difficult Sunlight: Poetry, Literacy, & Social Justice in Classroom & Community*

The authors have taken a very difficult thing—social justice—and worked it into teachable lessons. Classroom teachers will *get* this book, especially in this climate of intolerance and cruel bullying. More and more teachers are asking for cross-curriculum writing lessons, and the "Baseball Game Persona Poems" lesson fits that bill, delving into history, science, etc. The book has done a good job capturing the notion that teaching poetry is relevant and important.

—Bao-Long Chu, Writers in the Schools,
Houston, Texas

All teaching artists, veteran teachers who will work in partnership with them, and especially administrators in schools that host them should consider this a "must-read" text. Teachers will glean so much from this wonderful explanation and simple guiding directions. The lesson plans presented are complete and user friendly. They could be used in any school anywhere and make an impact. The rich vocabulary throughout the book pushed even me to look up words and increase my word bank!

—Paula Amaditz, elementary school principal (retired),
Forestburgh, New York

One of the most powerful and obvious strengths of the work are the two voices coming from uniquely different experiences (Black/White, female/male, Hip-Hop Generation/Boomer). Both writers bring not only a wealth of experience in urban, suburban, and rural schools, but also profound respect for the craft and for students and teachers as well. The manuscript is ripe with examples of respect and therefore a "listening" to the voices and experiences of the students. I have no doubt the book will be enthusiastically received for years to come.

—Jackie Warren-Moore, poet, playwright, and teaching artist,
Syracuse, New York

A real strength is the passion with which both writers write. It's interesting to read a book written by two different authors; I got the feeling I was getting a more well-rounded picture of the teaching artist's life by reading two perspectives. Their deep experiences as teaching artists come through. It's clear that both are excellent teachers who are very successful with students and teachers. Their lesson plans are clear, well written, and interesting.

—Mary Rechner, Literary Arts Writers in the Schools Programs,
Portland, Oregon

Our Difficult Sunlight

Our Difficult Sunlight

A Guide to Poetry, Literacy, & Social Justice in Classroom & Community

Georgia A. Popoff & Quraysh Ali Lansana

WITH A FOREWORD BY
Dr. Carol D. Lee

Teachers & Writers Collaborative
NEW YORK, NEW YORK

OUR DIFFICULT SUNLIGHT: A GUIDE TO POETRY, LITERACY,
& SOCIAL JUSTICE IN CLASSROOM & COMMUNITY

Library of Congress Cataloging-in-Publication Data
Popoff, Georgia A., 1953–
Lansana, Quraysh Ali, 1964–
Our difficult sunlight: a guide to poetry, literacy, & social justice in
classroom & community / Georgia A. Popoff & Quraysh Ali Lansana
ISBN-13: 978-0-915924-28-8 (ppk.-alk.paper)
ISBN-10: 0-915924-28-5 (ppk.-alk.paper)

2010942113

Teachers & Writers Collaborative
520 Eighth Avenue, Suite 2020
New York, NY 10018-6507

Cover and page design: Scribe Freelance | www.scribefreelance.com
Cover image: Joyce Owens

ACKNOWLEDGEMENTS

We appreciate Amy Swauger and the staff and Board of Directors of Teachers & Writers Collaborative for believing in us and this project.

Special thanks to Dr. Carol Lee for her foreword to this book, to Scribe Freelance for the design, and to Joyce Owens for the cover art.

We thank our research/editorial assistants Nick Tosoni, Jimmie Smith Jr., Shannon Lawrence VanSlyke, Derrick Harriell, and Amaris Howard.

Thank you to our peers who reviewed the manuscript for their insights, feedback, and support. We are grateful to Paula Amaditz, Bao-Long Chu, Nandi Comer, Mary Rechner, Bertha Rogers, and Jackie Warren-Moore.

My profound gratitude is offered to all of the students with whom I have shared poetry, adults and young people alike, over the years of my practice. To the teachers who have welcomed me to their classrooms, you are the heroes and my guidance. In particular, I thank the Enlarged City School District of Middletown, New York, as well as the school districts of Oswego, Syracuse, Fayetteville-Manlius, Liverpool, and Watkins Glen, New York, and Norwalk-La Mirada and Chico, California. In these schools I have practiced the art of teaching what I want to know about poetry. I am also thankful to the Downtown Writer's Center, Baldwinsville Public Library, Hillbrook Detention Center, and the countless community-based organizations where I have developed not just a following but a career as an artist educator.

My heart is grateful for all the friends and colleagues who have inspired, encouraged, and sustained me through this process and contributed to my work in general, including the extended Popoff family, Phil Alexander, Paula Amaditz, Marilyn Barletta, Becky Sue Bianco, Terry Blackhawk, Eric Booth, Dale Davis, Vita DeMarchi, Betsy DuBois, Linda Esterley, Martha Evans, Peggy Sperber Flanders, Keith Flynn, Bonnie French, Brian Goldblatt, Chuck

Harmon, MaryJo Heitkamp, Ryfkah Horwitz, Richard Lewis, Maria Marewski, Shari Mirman, Monica Minion, Linda Moore, Jennifer Pashley, Dawn Penniman, Susan Popoff, Bertha Rogers, Michael Sickler, Kimberly Swim, Sue Stonecash, Ellen Thornton, Jennifer Waters, Stephen Wright, the Judson Street neighbors, and the Rummikub crew who suffer my awkwardness with numbers. Hats off to the Children's Media Project and to all writing artists for working miracles every day.

To my own teachers, I always strive to honor you. In particular, I thank Lewis Turco, Paul Strong, Lewis Baldwin, Kathleen Crouch, Michael Fox, Walt Shepperd, Thelma Trotty-Selzer, and Gerhard Zeller. In memory of my parents, Betty Ann and Vladimir Popoff; where would I be if they had not seen the poet inside me?

Lastly, to my creative partner and dear friend, Quraysh Ali Lansana, thank you for this journey. It has been a remarkable testament to our commitment to the work as poets and in the world around us. You keep up with my overactive brain and you keep me grounded. You bring truth into every classroom in which you enter as you open hearts and minds to opportunity.

—Georgia A. Popoff

My thanks to the many teachers and students in Chicago, Kalamazoo, Middletown, and classrooms nationwide from whom, for the past 20 years, I have learned while sharing what I think I know.

Special thanks to my wife, Emily Hooper Lansana, Curriculum Coordinator for Theater and Literary Arts for Chicago Public Schools, and our sons Nile, Onam, Ari and Brooks for bearing with the late nights and cranky mornings. Also, much thanks to Dr. Rachel Lindsey, Dean, College of Arts and Sciences at Chicago State University, for her generous spirit and steadfast guidance. Additional thanks to Rosalyn Driver, Toni Asante Lightfoot, and the Mallette Family for much-needed support during the final stages of manuscript preparation.

My heartfelt thanks to the teachers that have shaped me, most notably: Gwendolyn Brooks, Haki R, Madhubuti, Lucille Clifton, Reginald Gibbons, Afaa Michael Weaver, Marilyn Nelson, Mark Doty, and Allan Wolf/Poetry Alive! My additional thanks to Mary Hawley and Mary Schafer, two amazing veterans of educational publishing, who furthered my understanding of a lesson plan.

Extra special thanks and maximum respect to Ms. Georgia Ann Popoff, whose brilliance and magic fill these pages and whose light is only brighter in the classrooms that inspire her mind and hand.

—Quraysh Ali Lansana

Our Difficult Sunlight: A Guide to Poetry, Literacy, & Social Justice in Classroom & Community was funded by grants from the National Endowment for the Arts and from the Simon and Eve Colin Foundation.

Teachers & Writers Collaborative programs are made possible in part by grants from the New York State Council on the Arts, the New York City Department of Cultural Affairs, Mayor Michael Bloomberg, and the New York City Council.

Teachers & Writers Collaborative is also grateful for support from Agnes Gund, Amazon.com, Axe-Houghton Foundation, Barnes & Noble, Booth Ferris Foundation, Bronx Council on the Arts, Bydale Foundation, Captivate Network, Center for Arts Education, Cerimon Fund, Consolidated Edison, Edward and Sally Van Lier Fund in the New York Commnunity Trust, E.H.A. Foundation, ING Financial Services, LEGO Children's Fund, Lily Auchincloss Foundation, LitTAP!, Lotos Foundation, Lower Manhattan Cultural Council, *New York Daily News*, Queens Council on the Arts, Rizzoli International Publications, Rockefeller Brothers Fund, Staten Island Foundation, Wachovia Wells Fargo Foundation, Washington Mutual Bank Foundation/JP Morgan Chase, and William Randolph Hearst Foundation.

Teachers & Writers Collaborative thanks the following for permission to reprint material in this book:

"The Good Man," "Boy Breaking Glass," and "The *Chicago Defender* Sends a Man to Little Rock" by Gwendolyn Brooks. Used by permission of Brooks Permissions.

"VII" and "VI" from *Liberation Narratives*, copyright 2009 by Haki R. Madhubuti, reprinted by permission of Third World Press, Inc., Chicago, Illinois.

"Purpose" by Janine Simon. Published in *The Best Teen Writing of 2006: The Scholastic Art & Writing Awards*. Copyright © 2006 Alliance for Young Artists & Writers, Inc. Reprinted by permission of Scholastic, Inc.

"Geometry," originally published in *The Yellow House on the Corner*, Carnegie Mellon University Press, Pittsburgh & London. © 1980 by Rita Dove. Reprinted by permission of the author.

"Knoxville, Tennessee" from *Black Feeling, Black Talk, Black Judgment* by Nikki Giovanni. Copyright © 1968, 1970 by Nikki Giovanni. Reprinted by permission of HarperCollins Publishers.

"Trails" by Ann Silsbee, used by permission of Red Hen Press.

"Bear Song" by Kay Run. © Kay Ryan, used by permission of the poet.

"eighth grade" by Quraysh Ali Lansana. Used by permission of the author.

"Haiti in 3-D" and "Purpose of Life" by Purpose of Life Poetry Ensemble. Used by permission of the authors.

"seventy-first & king drive" from *southside rain* by Quraysh Ali Lansana. Used by permission of the author.

TABLE OF CONTENTS

Force our poor sense into your logics, lend
superlatives and prudence: to extend
our judgment—through the terse and diesel day;
to
singe, smite, beguile our own bewilderments away.
Teach barterers the money of your star.
In the time of detachment, in the time of cold, in this time
tutor our difficult sunlight.
Rouse our rhyme.

—Gwendolyn Brooks, from
The Good Man

FOREWORD

---

*An Exceeding Sun: A Poetic Pedagogy for
Liberation and Personal Growth*

Dr. Carol D. Lee

I have long believed that our great writers have the gift of second sight,
unique envisionments of the conundrums of what it means to grow (or
not) over time as humans. What perhaps distinguishes them from other
insightful artists is how, as Ralph Ellison describes, they "jump into the
breaks [of life] and look around" with language as their immersion. They
dig deep into the contours and possibilities of language, often turning the
ordinary into the extraordinary.

Language almost always has possibilities of duality, of multiplicity, of
nuance. For example, African-American English is replete with creative uses
of metaphor, symbolism, satire, double entendre. Speakers of African-
American English are socialized into placing great value on playing with
language, on the aesthetic possibilities of words as sounds, rhythms, and
meanings. Speakers of Spanglish code switch between languages with verve
and insight into the special meanings each language makes possible.

Verbal word play is a common practice across language communities.
Common verbal play is a bridge where the canonical and the everyday
intersect. Ironically, schools rarely help students traverse back and forth
across these bridges (Lee, 2007). More often than not, popular culture and
literary movements that aim to inspire and uplift intensify movement back
and forth from the everyday and the canonical. Langston Hughes and Zora
Neale Hurston complemented the chorus of Marcus Garvey in Black
America of the 1930s and 1940s; Amiri Baraka, Sonia Sanchez, Haki
Madhubuti, and Nikki Giovanni sparked a Black Arts Movement that
walked alongside the Black Power and Civil Rights Movements in the
1960s and 1970s. In both of these examples, the literature was emboldened
with political activism that inspired people to resist and to transform the
constraints on their opportunities.

We live again today in the midst of a new blossoming of language peppered with visions of empowerment, a blossoming that lives on the written page, on the digital screen, in word-smithing public performances, and in the rhythms of Hip Hop. There are myriad petals in this blossoming, from poets such as Quraysh Ali Lansana and Georgia Popoff, who authored this magnificent volume, to Hip-Hop artists such as Common and Wyclef Jean, to the elementary and grade school students whose creative words pop from the pages of this volume. In the current and historical exemplars, attention to deep self-reflection through aesthetic play with language is the constant.

Lansana and Popoff are stunning poets who have not only invested their lives in their own poetic craft, but who have also utilized their residencies in K-12 schools to help young people examine their inner selves and public circumstances through writing. In this volume, they strive to make public the pedagogy they have been able to develop through this school-based work in the hope that other writers and educators can learn from what they have been able to accomplish. They explicate this poetic pedagogy through narratives of exemplary cases of their practice. In these cases, we meet young people wrestling with problematic and complex challenges. We can see through the conversations they have with Lansana and Popoff, and through the young peoples' writing that explodes off the page, how this pedagogy evolved and what it looks like on the ground.

Lansana and Popoff do not create a Pollyannaish portrait, but rather confront the many difficulties of doing this work. There are many stakeholders who can learn from these portraits: parents, teachers, school administrators, humanities organizations, and other writers. The lessons for each of these stakeholders may be different and require different ways of adapting, embellishing, expanding the fundamentals of this pedagogy. But underlying what Lansana and Popoff are trying to accomplish is finding ways to enable young people to interrogate their own voices, to learn to dance with language, and to connect with the broader issues of their times, issues that can and do help to shape who and what these young people will become.

In reading this volume, I heard the voice of a dear friend to both Lansana and me, the magnificent poet Gwendolyn Brooks. At the height of the Black Arts Movement and its sister struggles, the Black Power and Civil Rights Movements, Ms. Brooks wrote the volume *In the Mecca* with poems of terse language wreaking with deep philosophy and politics. Among them is the following:

Boy Breaking Glass
To Marc Crawford
from whom the commission

Whose broken window is a cry of art
(success, that winks aware
as elegance, as a treasonable faith)
is raw: is sonic: is old-eyed première.
Our beautiful flaw and terrible ornament.
Our barbarous and metal little man.

"I shall create! If not a note, a hole.
If not an overture, a desecration."

Full of pepper and light
and Salt and night and cargoes.

"Don't go down the plank
if you see there's no extension.
Each to his grief, each to
his loneliness and fidgety revenge.
Nobody knew where I was and now I am no longer there."

The only sanity is a cup of tea.
The music is in minors.

Each one other
is having different weather.

"It was you, it was you who threw away my name!
And this is everything I have for me."

Who has not Congress, lobster, love, luau,
the Regency Room, the Statue of Liberty,
runs. A sloppy amalgamation.
A mistake.
A cliff.
A hymn, a snare, and an exceeding sun.

The idea of a "broken window [as] a cry of art" seems to me the theme of this volume. The young people we meet *In the Mecca* are the young people we meet in this volume. The possibility of art to buttress "our barbarous and metal little man," to create a note rather than a hole, an overture rather than a desecration is what I think Lansana and Popoff aim to do, and to help others learn to do. And what is liberating is that they understand that the conundrums of the "barbarous and metal little man" can be found across human communities. The challenges of life are not unique niches of racial and ethnic ghettoes. As my friend and colleague Dr. Margaret Beale Spencer of the University of Chicago so wisely notes, to be human is to be at risk. The task of life course development is to learn to wrestle with that risk and to rise.

Lansana and Popoff have named this volume *Our Difficult Sunlight*. I like to pull from Ms. Brooks and think of their work as "an exceeding sun."

Our HuManifesto: A Prologue, a Position Statement, a Pair of Poets Talkin'

Georgia A. Popoff & Quraysh Ali Lansana

VII.

if the world loses elephants,
dolphins, polar bears, frogs, trees,
the ability of the majority to do good,
clean water, prayer & meditation in all languages,
if the world loses love across borders,
honest vegans & vegetarians
a mother's love, a father's caring,
children dancing to knowledge & colors,
artists not lying for money, privilege or fame,
if the world loses books, newspapers,
clear thinkers, practical doers, poets
promising futures for the great majority, rainforests.
A world vocabulary that accents yes & possibilities
rather than no and you can't do that,
if the world loses the great apes, schools,
giraffes, salmon, the coral reefs, insects,
worms, organic farmers, compost, green tea,
workers who use their hands
to build & repair stuff, north and south poles,
teachers, people of faith, engineers,
wheat-grass, carrot juice, oatmeal and seven grain bread.

If the world loses you and water,
yes, precious you and the daily taste of life

it finally means that
we've lost butterflies yesterday
and failed our children.

-Haki R. Madhubuti,
from *Liberation Narratives*

Like a living thing, this book has been rooting in our minds and mouths for more than a decade. We are poets and colleagues who share a common focus: the craft of language that stresses conscious choice for purposeful communication and connection between reader and writer as humans. Within these pages, we hope to articulate our ongoing dialogue of mutual practice and approaches to reading, writing, and teaching poetry, a conversation based on our individual and shared sensibilities regarding:

- The art and craft of poetry;

- The relevance of poetry to culture and society;

- The power of language to motivate or provide impetus for change on the personal level, as well as the grand scale;

- The opportunity to promote poetry as a creative art, a learning tool, and an imaginative experience in public schools and community-based programs; and

- Poetry as literature—inventing with language to create windows into worlds and cultures other than one's own.

Our Difficult Sunlight: A Guide to Poetry, Literacy, & Social Justice in Classroom & Community is structured in a way that combines our shared thought with our individual practices and approaches that speak to the main themes of each section of the book. These sections open with a collaborative introduction to establish a scope and context for the individually-authored essays that follow. We also provide comprehensive lesson plans building on the content of each section. This book is intended to be resource guide, method, model, and premise. The lesson plans may be adapted and revised as relevant to the individual educator's curriculum, needs, and grade level.

Our structure permits us to share our similar vision, but reflects the ways our backgrounds make our individual essays and views distinct. Georgia is of the 1950s Baby Boom at the wane of deep segregation and a time of great social upheaval; she was a teen during the Vietnam War and early years of the Women's Movement. Quraysh was born in the middle of the Civil Rights Era and came of age on the cusp of Hip Hop. Georgia is of European descent; Quraysh is of African-American and Cherokee blood. We believe we were, in many ways, the young poets we teach now. We will, no doubt, continue our conversation beyond the pages of this book.

If we were to be before the bench in a "court of poetic law," this book would serve as the brief, stating our case for the value of poetry in education. We believe that the writing arts have the capacity to fit into every aspect of learning in the classroom, at the community center, and in the living room. We also believe that the writing arts should be included in the learning standards and curriculum as a fine-arts discipline.

Poetry is a living, breathing animal, and the kind of animal it is varies depending upon who you are and where you are—it is adaptable, topical, and transformative. Poetry may help students see differently; language is the tool or vehicle for the expression of that different sight. Our work involves instilling students with a love of language, showing them that language has the power to change minds and that it may contribute to self-awareness and transformation.

Becoming an effective writer organically builds personal power. Self-esteem and confidence result from the ability to organize and articulate one's thoughts and knowledge. We believe the more language one knows, the more power one has to make better choices on the journey through life. Much of life is negotiation—on the street, in the workplace, in the home. Having a strong command of both written and oral language positions young people for success in everything from applying to college, to interviewing for jobs, to making wise decisions about loan applications.

The value of writing and reading go far beyond life's practicalities, though. For years within some arts-in-education dialogues, particularly within arts-education advocacy, many have argued that the writing arts should not be included among the fine-arts disciplines because "the students get creative writing with ELA [English language arts] anyway." Throughout the nation, school districts and state learning standards isolate the writing arts from their companion creative disciplines. This approach diminishes an understanding of writing as a creative art form first, a literary construct second.

Often as we visit teachers in their own environments, they are eager for any ideas that will support their own lesson planning in writing, especially poetry. Teachers are looking for resources and strategies that move beyond the standard unit of study and the potential for the ordinary, even the routine. Many of us remember poetry as being dull, uninventive, obscure, and outdated. Some teachers have admitted to us that they are either intimidated by having to teach poetry or just plain do not like the form.

Our intention for this book is to provide colleagues with a variety of elements to bolster their own practices. The first section of the book, "Demystifying the Poem: Poems as Tools for Comprehension and Expression," presents a platform for engaging with a poem through a tiered inquiry process that empowers both teachers and students to develop and trust their own interpretations of the work. "Poetry and Curriculum Connections: Inquiry and Reflection in the Core Subjects" offers essays with the theme of poetry as it relates to general literacy, improved reading comprehension, and core content instruction. "Poetry and Diversity: Language, Emotion, and Shared Experience" explores creativity, self-expression, acceptance among diverse communities, and social justice.

Because we care to do more than simply pontificate, we strove to develop a structure that furnishes practical applications as well as food for thought; lessons, exercises, recommended poems, and resources along with theory. Though the essays and lesson plans presented in any given section may appear to address a particular grade level or age group, we encourage the classroom teachers or teaching artists who read this book to adapt the lessons to suit the cognitive levels of whatever ages they are guiding. We believe that each of our poetic processes is pertinent to most age groups, and we recognize that educators and teaching writers possess the skill to adapt these lessons to suit their own instruction. [**Note:** Additional lesson plans and other resources can be found on the Teachers & Writers Collaborative website: www.twc.org/sunlight.]

Some may take our statements as pie-in-the-sky pedagogy. Some may believe that we are not conscious of the extreme limitations of today's classroom. Our politics may be bold but they are heartfelt. Our pedagogy is based on years of trial and error, as well as the countless examples of excellent teaching we have witnessed throughout our careers.

We have summarized our core beliefs in the six "poetic premises" listed below:

POETIC PREMISE ONE: *A FINE BALANCE*

A statement commonly attributed to Langston Hughes is that in creating poetry, "The prerequisite to writing is having something to say." With this in mind, we recognize the importance of reminding students that everything is significant, if viewed through the proper lens. Writing is not about being *deep, meaningful, and profound*; it is about the conscious act of participating, observing, reporting, and reflecting the world in which we live.

> We believe:
>
> - in artistic and creative integrity,
>
> - in craft and aesthetic,
>
> - in knowing our history (honoring those upon whose shoulders we stand), and
>
> - in a balance of message and prosody.

The craft of a poem should not suffer because of its message or intent. We do not place one value over the other. They are of equal import. Additionally, a poem must work as well on the page as it does to the ear. If it works for one, but not the other, the poem fails.

POETIC PREMISE TWO: *A DEEPER CONNECTION*

We believe that poetry is a conduit to worlds beyond and within us. By elevating our conscious familiarity with the world in which we live, we can touch those hard-to-reach places in our collective and individual humanity. Poetry encourages its audience to commune with the magical, the miracle, and to discern the mundane as beyond our own making. This strengthens our being. This leaves behind the need for answers to unanswerable questions. Poetry is the language of mystery and imagination.

There was a time when poetry was the primary chronicle of the human experience. The voice of the voiceless, poetry spoke truth to power, gave language to the lips in our mirror's image. The stories of the *djelis*, West-African historians, and of European jesters carried the tales and follies of community folk life both within and across boundaries and borderlines.

In the 1970s, while Lewis Turco taught Georgia and other young writers studying at SUNY (State University of New York) Oswego, he spoke of the tradition of poets, reaching back to the pagan shamans who held and spoke the incantations for the people, a rhythm that has maintained for ages.

It was Galway Kinnell's practice to have his poetry-writing classes at New York University listen to a recording of tree frogs. That is what his students, including Quraysh, did for an hour, listened to frogs. Some folks sneered, some folks refused to take it seriously or listen clearly. Some folks went to sleep. It is possible that Galway wanted poets to understand that arc and hue and shading are different types of music. The lyric of tree frogs can inform how we, as poets, work with the musicality of language.

Michael Fox, a former art professor at SUNY Oswego, designed a lecture class for first-year art students that centered a great deal of its lessons on seeing and critical thinking, presented in a series of terrific slide shows. One lecture titled "What Color is Snow?" proved that light and color may be as layered and patterned as any weaving. Images of blue snowbanks and gray storms, lavender waves of snow, sheets of silver and gold flakes, in morning light or evening glow flashed as students discovered snow is anything but white. Noticing became a much different act than merely seeing.

As with the visual arts, to the poet, any lesson in noticing provides a profound imprint on artistic process, even on one's mode of existence. A poet who is blind or deaf will "notice" through all the other senses. It is necessary for any poet to move beyond the visual, upon which most sighted poets base their imagery, for a fuller life and a more poignant poem to reflect those moments, both big and small, that comprise a worldview.

POETIC PREMISE THREE: *A METAPHOR FOR GROWTH AND DEVELOPMENT*

Poetry is not a static or arbitrary entity, not within the individual poem or poet, and not within society or culture. It is beyond analysis and it never stays the same. Poetry is organic and evolving within the creative process, for the reader, for the poet, and within community. The individual poem grows from the moment of creative inception through drafts and conscious revision, sometimes even after first publication. The poet grows in self-knowledge through the artistic process.

The lineage and craft of poetry change from writer to writer and through generations. Language itself is ever-evolving. According to the French feminist writer and intellectual, Hélène Cixous, "When I write, language remembers...I inscribe an additional memory in language—a memory in progress." The dictionary is not carved in stone. It breathes and sheds its skin, then grows a new lexicon as we drop words from use and create new ones. Languages are discovered and others become extinct throughout the globe as a matter of course.

Poetry and metaphor amplify critical skills and enhance a holistic education through imaging content, then drawing inference from and reflecting that content. Poetry as metaphor, in terms of our pedagogy for the "full book bag" of all curriculum content is, in and of itself, an aesthetic and comprehensive approach to addressing all subject areas. Poetry, by design and through metaphor, is a magnifying glass, a telescope, an earpiece, and a microphone.

POETIC PREMISE FOUR: *ART AS IMPETUS*

Art should move us to think, not tell us what to think. We have enough preachers, politicians, and pundits to do that. Though there is always something that the poet wants us to discern, the poem demands of its audience interpretation, self-reflection, interaction, and application. The poem must be artistically as solid as its message. There is a difference between reportage and description. There is also a difference between didacticism and dissidence. As art, the poem must be able to stand on its own as an independent entity that invokes response from its audience.

POETIC PREMISE FIVE: *SOCIAL JUSTICE AND RIGHTEOUS INDIGNATION*

There was a time when poetry was a primary vehicle for dissidence and protest. Poetry bore evidence of injustice and oppression; for those who questioned authority and did not turn a blind eye to inequities, it was an outlet for communication. Poetry is inclusive; there is resonance in poetic language that allows disparate peoples to find commonalities and a sense of unity, a place of belonging. Poetry may be a political act as well as a personal megaphone.

POETIC PREMISE SIX: *THE VOICE OF THE VOICELESS*

We both have noticed countless workshop participants for whom self-expression was new territory, one in which they had not previously felt privileged or safe. Whether or not students read their poems aloud, the fact that they have faced their thoughts, fears, and dreams, then committed them to paper, is liberating. Writing a poem is a courageous act that validates and claims ownership of one's thoughts and beliefs. This bearing witness of self can happen in the park, the jail unit, the school library, on the playground, or in the basement of any house of worship. The home is often the place where self-reflection and proclamation are most stifled, where the cycle of silence begins. Can a journal of poems become a sanctuary? Will the poem give authority to one's heart?

Our commitment as teaching poets is driven by the desire to reduce the trepidation people often experience in connecting with verse. We strive to communicate and amplify poetry as a key element of a quality and thoughtful life. Developing pedagogy to support that mission has led us through the "tried and true," bumps and scrapes, frustrations and joys, as well as a lot of time on the road and in self-reflection. What is it that we truly want to impart? How do we truly believe poetry works in society? How does poetry serve each of us? These questions root us in our shared practice and are the source for this book. We hope we give you something that smoothes your journey and affirms your own mission.

DEMYSTIFYING THE POEM

Poems as Tools for Comprehension and Expression

INTRODUCTION

※

Georgia A. Popoff & Quraysh Ali Lansana

It is our shared belief that poetry is an effective and under-utilized tool for developing competent literacy, including reading comprehension skills, at all grade levels. The very nature of how the poem is constructed—the formatting of sentences into lines and stanzas—fosters a more conscious approach to reading, slowing the reader down by breaking thoughts into smaller, more digestible phrases.

Our pedagogy is based on this tempered investigation and "digestion," which enhance the process of reading and writing poems. We believe the process of writing poetry is often dismissed or made secondary to the race toward the end product. This may have a great deal to do with how the public-school environment has been reduced to a constant drive to prepare students for standardized assessments. This climate tends to quantify, rather than qualify, learning. The end result, the culminating event, supersedes process-based inquiry that supports development of critical-thinking skills.

When poetry is viewed as a "product," rather than a process of both critical and creative thinking, it reduces the poem to a "thing." The outcome becomes more important than the journey of discovery that leads students and educators to that outcome. The elegance of detailing the elements that make poetry magical, the craft that transforms inspiration into metaphor, image, and communication, are often subservient to the culminating event—an acceptable final product—and subsequent evaluations.

Think of the poem as a planet. Ways that the poem may be expressed and/or experienced become its satellites, including:

- Reading the poem to oneself,

- Reading the poem aloud,

- Memorizing and reciting the poem,

- Spoken word and performance poetry, and

- Hip Hop as a genre of contemporary poetry.

These satellites are all in service to the planet, all revolving to make the source and essence of the poem tangible.

This is not to suggest that we are either purists or uptight academicians. We appreciate diversity of poetic form and expression. It is possible to offer templates that incorporate elements of prosody, and this approach may result in students crafting delightful and surprising poems. However, we believe it is more effective to encourage students to take poetic journeys of their own design. Although it is not likely that we will turn out legions of prolific poets who make the long trek from inspiration through the stages of revision, reinvestigation, and deliberation, we may motivate a young writer to share what the morning sun looks like as it rises over the roof of a Bronx apartment building, the fence between two houses in South Central Los Angeles, or the barn silo the schoolbus passes each morning. We share the conviction that everyone can write a poem. There are some who will shine in the light of this art or discover a strength that was previously unrecognized but, through the steps we present, a basis for success for all is established.

In our experience, many people feel inept in relating to and understanding poetry. We have met people who equate a single reading of a poem with an intelligence test. If the reader is "smart," the skies open up with choirs of affirmation, accolades for the reader's "wisdom." If the poem "boggles" the reader, that person is just "too dumb" to ascertain the exalted meaning. How unfortunate that such a wondrous and complex art form has been reduced to an "intell-o-meter." The belief that a poem has one clear meaning is a lie that denies many the pleasures of language and its crafted message.

As teaching poets, we have made conscious decisions to empower students at any age level with these basic tenets:

- Language is an enthralling and malleable asset that fosters a sense of confidence and capacity.

- Individuals can be guided to observe the world in a manner different than they normally employ.

- The poem is a form of communication of that new vision, a method of expressing the personal interpretation of a worldview.

- Poetry is a vehicle for accessing acceptance and understanding of differences among peoples, cultures, and backgrounds.

- Poetry is the only art form intended to be received in two manners: from the printed page and by the ear.

- Through continued engagement with poetry, an individual can become both a more adept reader and a more empathetic human.

- The essence the poet wanted to convey is discovered through repeated examinations of the poem. These visitations encourage patient investigation of the work that, in turn, strengthens competency in inference and interpretation.

- By virtue of the personal interpretative aspect of poetic inference, there are no wrong answers if the person receiving the poem can cite evidence to support understanding and interpretation from the content.

- The pleasure of such discovery is a mystery to unravel; the excitement of turning the content of language into a new vision is joyous.

Reading is more than decoding words on the page. It is travel through the unknown. Each time people to read, be it an article in the *New Yorker*, *National Enquirer*, or *Popular Mechanics*, or *The Norton Anthology of Poetry*, their curiosity may be sparked, spurring them to further exploration. The unique format of a poem coaxes the reader to slow down. The goal of getting to the end of the page or the column is less pressing than immersion in the music of alliteration and rhythm, or the emotion and connotation of words in collaboration that compose the poem.

MINING FOR MEANING

◼

Poetry as Archaeology

Georgia A. Popoff & Quraysh Ali Lansana

The process of reading poems exercises the mind in much the same way as playing the word game *Boggle*. Just as the eyes connect the letter patterns on the game grid more quickly as one continues to play, inference and meaning emerge more readily from content when a poem is read thoughtfully and multiple times. Layers of poetic images reveal secrets, in the same way an archaeologist sifts through layers of soil for pottery shards and evidence of past civilizations. The poem is not intended to be read just once. It is not the drive-thru menu at a Jack in a Box. It is a piece of art in which every word is a deliberate choice and has earned its way into the whole.

In classrooms, we often hear students being asked to "analyze" a poem. This is a highly intimidating approach to engaging with poetry. It reflects a false assumption that students will develop the competency to discover meaning and insight by simply decoding the words, as if a poem were an equation.

This is not to say the elements of poetry taught in the traditional classroom poetry unit are not important to understanding. For example, alliteration is a key component of poetry's music and, thus, a memorable device in a poem, but it rarely helps a student connect to the poet's intention or inspiration. Similarly, identifying onomatopoeia or poetic meter does not inform student inference about meaning. The mechanics of the writing process are comprised of an array of literary devices that adds to the sensory attributes of a poem, but they are not the keys to the highway of understanding. In fact, few poets sit down to write with a formulaic approach to the emotion they seek to express to others. It is a much more immediate and compulsive act. We often do not make conscious decisions to write about something; we are blindsided by the need to record our point of view or inspiration. We will likely use the vehicle of a particular form or literary device to support our muse, but our process is much more organic than analytical.

On the other hand, we recognize that a poem is a terrific tool for recognizing parts of speech and grammar. Poems can also provide a different angle on thematic content in curricular areas like history or science. Poetry transcends time and culture, and a poem can transport a student to a distant geographic location or historic era, or to a specific emotion. The poem can cause questions to fly or answers to be derived. Most important, a poem is a bridge between humans—through poetry, hearts and minds connect in ways that strengthen both writer and audience. Humans are not so alone when the words of a poem, and the underlying emotion or observation, are shared and recognizable.

A poet molds language into form and does so with the intention of audience—someone to read or listen to the work. Poets strive to say something of value with the expectation of connection to and reliance upon the reader or audience member to receive the communication. This drives poets to publish and perform. It drives poets to teach. And it drives us crazy.

How do we know that the "thing" we've produced is a poem? This is where the mechanics of poetry come into play. Is it evident that metaphor is at work? Is a connection being drawn between dissimilar things that become quite logical partners in understanding meaning? Will a reader or listener recognize the economy of language and conscious word choice meant to indicate a certain image or belief? Is there a deliberate structure that furthers interpretation of the words, such as line and stanza development? All of these considerations distinguish verse from prose.

Compare the poem versus prose discussion to orange juice. Many enjoy a refreshing glass of juice with breakfast. Many of us purchase frozen concentrate and then dilute it three-to-one to reformulate the beverage. Look at the full pitcher as the personal essay, the long journal entry, the short story. Consider the cardboard tube with tin bottom and top full of thick orange goo as the poem. The concentration of effective language—the distillation of words to essential vocabulary—is the source of the poem's artistic integrity and its impact on others.

Does the poem come easily for those of us who self-identify as poet? The myth may be that we are anointed with the capacity to put pen to paper or fingers to keyboard and, after a flurry of activity and dexterity, produce a perfect poem. We are satisfied, fingers poised for the next poem, now that this one has run its course. If only it were that easy. In fact, the act of poetry is an exploration and discovery of which the first draft is merely the map, the blueprint, maybe even the light on the miner's hat. We then get to sculpt the form in the way Michelangelo released the bodies of his subjects from slabs of stone; we select words the way Van Gogh chose colors and brushes for a particular texture and energy. We revisit and revise our thoughts often. We work it and we work it hard, though this work is our play. We often use the word "play" in our teaching to encourage students to be diligent and invested in self-expression. We ask them to "play with the thesaurus." We ask them to strive in ways similar to an athlete training or an archaeologist sifting for relics.

In his September 2009 address to US students[1], President Barack Obama challenged them not to hand in the first draft of written assignments. He asked them to pilot the work through the stages that lead not only to a better grade, but also to greater expression and subsequent understanding by the person reading the work. He was asking students to develop a work ethic, to invest pride in their efforts.

Students' lack of the habit of hard work can be the greatest hurdle any of us engaged in instruction must overcome. The two pleas: *Am I done?* and *Is this good?* echo through the aisles of desks like a song sung incessantly in the round. Most frequently the answer to the first question is *Maybe, but probably not,* or *And then what happened?* We can usually answer the second question with *Good start* as we point out opportunities to "kick it up a notch," to quote the "street poet" and TV cooking show host Emeril Lagasse. Students want to be done quickly and praised highly. Don't we all? By using poetry to encourage a slower, more deliberate process, we teach patience, pride, self-awareness, self-esteem, and taking responsibility for a job well done, along with knowing verb from noun, past from present tense.

Poems were part of daily life long before the invention of the camera or radio. The history of poetry predates Gutenberg and the printing press and

---

[1] "Back-to-School Message to America's Students," September 8, 2009.

legions of monks with quills in hand; in fact, it predates written language. The shaman lifting face to the heavens to incant prayers in verse was the first of our lineage. The bards wandering from one distant clan or village to the next with news and family tales are our ancestors. We preserve our history and strive to induct new initiates into the genealogy as we promote poetry to others. It is not necessary for each student to become an accomplished poet, but he will learn lessons that may inform future writing tasks in school and beyond. We also hope to create new audiences. Reading poetry and, even more, attempting to write a poem expands command of language, or at the least it expands students' vocabularies.

Developing skill in recognizing metaphor and literary devices prompts inquiry that can lead to a wide range of discoveries. For instance, we can enter a poem written in 1765 and immerse ourselves in the substance of situations, pains, and joys of that era. None of us can fully understand what life was like in the 1700s. But we can connect to it via our personal interpretations of the poetic elements that detail the human experience 300 years ago. The contextual substance of a poem from that era may require research for complete understanding. Still, the poem itself provides footholds to secure the reader's engagement with the original message, and empathy for its author and/or characters depicted in the poem. Drawing conclusions from sensory prompts, keen observation, and critical thinking leads to an aptitude for creative problem-solving and effective communication, as well as improved skill in drawing inference from content. Additionally, the brain exercises its capacity to move from its visual "vocabulary" of images to language, and back again, through the exploration of a poem.

We will never all agree that every poem or poet is "good," any more than we may agree on a movie's merit, or all like the same piece of music or painting on a gallery wall. There are too many factors that contribute to different tastes. We can agree, though, on effective methods to enter a work of art in order to make an informed decision about how and why we view it as we do. In helping students learn to articulate their views of a poem, the question *What does this poem mean?* Is a less valid construct than *What do you believe the poet wants you to think, feel, and/or believe from these words?*

The first question is a *STOP* sign to most students. The second is a cruising lane on the highway from which a traveler observes the landscape and follows the road signs. The first intimidates with its demand for the correct response. The second empowers the person encountering the poem to develop a confident argument that is grounded in critical thought and personal interpretation. This encourages learning that is rooted in inference. A simple change in perspective from analysis to investigation makes reading and interpreting a poem more active and personal. Moving from asking students to break down a poem as a formula to challenging them to uncover its meaning layer by layer is only a shift in focus for the teacher. As this method is revised for the individual classroom, making it habit improves chances for continued success. (See the lesson plan, "Recipe for a Simple Start: Poem of the Week," on page 89 for one approach.)

As teaching artists, we are often more concerned with creative and critical process than outcome. We hope students will find joy in the process, and seeing them experience that joy is enough for us. However, in the current climate of education and the subsequent focus on standards and assessment, we do our best to accommodate both in our plans and curricula. With a longer-term partnership between a school and teaching writer, there will likely be a well-founded evaluation process for all elements of the program, students, teachers, and resident artists. Frequently, however, in a short-term residency (three to five days), there is little formal assessment or evaluation of student performance and response, much less that of either the professional educator, or the work of teaching artists in residence. This is most often due to time and/or funding constraints. To their credit, teachers recognize and honor that there are times that learning as pure enjoyment is a primary goal; attachment to product is less important in that moment of satisfaction.

In addition, assessing student poetry is always tricky due to the subjectivity inherent in any individual's response to reading a poem. While we keep this subjectivity in mind as we teach, we strive to affirm rather than deflate student confidence in competent writing. Georgia has composed four simple questions to pose to students for self-assessment:

- Did you meet the criteria we agreed to for this assignment?

- Are you satisfied with what you created?

- Are you proud of your writing and your efforts?

- Did you enjoy yourself?

If the answers to all four questions are *yes* and the effort is evident, the young writers have fully satisfied her expectations.

We believe this is a golden age for poetry, perhaps the first since the 50s and 60s, when the Beats, the Black Arts Movement, and the poetry of other sociological movements gave voice to innovation and marginalized citizens. Some of this resurgence has to do with the birth and long life of Hip-Hop culture and its stepchild, spoken word. However, do those immersed in Hip Hop and spoken word fully comprehend they are actually returning to their roots? As the young rapper "spits" on the street corner or the spoken-word artist orates from the stage, the same breath that fed fires with verse a thousand years ago is re-emerging. As the young poet spills his broken heart onto ruled paper and then from an open-mic stage, we can hear Rumi's "Love Dogs" howling in the distance. The angry young woman proclaiming in rhyme that she will be no one's bitch is likely carrying the same tone of protest expressed in the translation of cuneiform tablets of the Sumerian woman poet, Enheduanna, as she pounded her outrage into clay in 2300 BCE.

In spite of all the media swirling in, through, and around us, humans still need to be heard. The quietest student may produce the most powerful poetry, perhaps simply because that student finds safety on the page that speaking aloud does not permit. Is the poetic discourse of Wanda Coleman any different in source and substance than the middle-school student often written up for disciplinary referral who sits at the library computer for an entire lunch period to release three pages of verse and simile that speak her pain? Is it possible to build on that visceral reaction to nurture that creative being into even more vivid ways to communicate her rage? The goal is to help writers get beyond the self-congratulatory into a discernment of craft.

The Power of Language

◾

The Struggle Continues

Georgia A. Popoff

> Let me make this very simple for you. Words are
> power. The more words you know and can recognize,
> use, define, understand, the more power you will have
> as a human being. Hear me when I say this. The more
> language you know, the more likely it is that no one
> can get over on you. This is the most practical reason I
> can offer as to why you want to listen to me speak to
> you about poetry.
>
> —Georgia A. Popoff,
> introductory class comments

After 10 years in schools, and while working with teen writers in community settings for five years before that, I realize that I need to present a very tangible reason for students to engage in my thinking, my process, and my enthusiasm for poetry. The lines above exemplify my initial approach to middle- and high-school classrooms. I have often found it necessary to use my skills from the years in which I sold insurance to "get the close" when I enter a classroom of young people who likely have little interest in poetry, or so they believe. I stand before them, another adult with expectations; an adult who is not only old enough to be their mother but their grandmother; an adult with perhaps a different skin tone, hair color, ethnic or cultural background, perhaps a different first language.

Although it may seem we have very little in common, I am compelled to help students see past our differences to the sameness we share as humans. And then, once we have established a trust, a connection, I want to encourage them to embrace poetry, either by reading a poem or by creating one of their own. I hope to help them see that poetry is already an active agent in their lives, through the music they listen to, the advertising they are surrounded by, and the very words they know and use daily. I strive to point out that language is a beautiful and fluid thing. I intend to infect as many as possible with an unbridled awe for what language can accomplish, from its basic musicality to its most terrifying ability to control our every action.

I want my students to understand that it is quite simple to hide behind the language we speak to each other, the codes lurking in how we speak, the imprints of media and pop culture. It is critical for them to develop the skill to interpret language more fully and to protect themselves with words first, weapons and force last. I want them to believe it is possible to change somebody's mind, even change society, if they can effectively utilize words. There are countless examples throughout politics and history.

When I ask a class to name those who support my premise, generally the first response is Dr. Martin Luther King Jr. Some astute students will cite Malcolm X, John F. Kennedy, Nelson Mandela, or Mahatma Gandhi. If I then counter with the challenge to cite someone who changed society in negative ways, Hitler is unfailingly the first name spoken. Again, the astute may count Stalin, Trotsky, Mao, Joseph McCarthy.

Sometimes I find myself standing in front of a class of reluctant, even recalcitrant learners, and I have to work harder to help them understand why they should engage in our shared exploration of language. Often there is ethnic diversity among the students that permits a short demonstration, the most relevant I have stumbled upon yet. I point to the male students of European descent, those with "white" skin, and ask them to stand. Then I present my well-worn notion to the rest of the class: *170 or so years ago, these are the only ones among us who would be permitted to be in this classroom. Now, tell me why.* Young people must be reminded that their school day is no light endeavor. All women as well as men of color once were oppressed by education being withheld from us. Neither group had the right to property, or to knowledge. To learn was a subversive act. It still is.

I tell my students that their grandparents, even their parents, may have marched and fought for the right to learn, and to learn next to each other, side by side in the same classroom. They may have been hosed, beaten, arrested, drummed out of neighborhoods for their insistence on the right to an education. Or they may have parents or grandparents on the other side of the argument. Perhaps some students' grandparents were vocal about maintaining schools separated by race. Maybe their mothers did not attend a university because they were expected to marry or care for family members. Some of their fathers may have been forced by circumstance or parentage into factories or onto farm equipment instead of college. They may have left school to sign up or been drafted into the military.

As I continue to dialogue with the class, if my point of view has not already prodded a lively discussion on the subjects of oppression, our innate intelligence, and the right to express it, then I advance to the next level of illustration: I count the number of males of color in the room and divide by four. Then I ask that number of young men to stand. Like trees in a pasture these young men are metaphors themselves, exemplars of dead men walking.

Many of today's young people face another future. I ask my students to consider the national statistic cited repeatedly in the media: one in four young men of color will be incarcerated or die a violent death before reaching age 25. One of the fastest growing industries is the penal system, perhaps one of the most reliable sources of employment in the United States. Think of all the jobs: architects, engineers, construction workers, truck drivers, prison guards, cafeteria staff, social workers, parole officers, judges, police, trash haulers, uniform factory sewers. This is the cost of devalued public education and the lack of literacy in America. And to me, the prison system appears built to perpetuate itself; the job machine keeps itself well oiled. I say to the class, *There are those who are heavily invested in your failure, and they are not your parents, your teachers, your principals, or your superintendent. They may be the jailer or the recruiter. The politician or the undertaker.*

When I voice my radical opinions to students, we have another opportunity for animated discussion, providing me the space to add these considerations: *What if you embraced your education as a form of civil disobedience? What if you graduate and go to college, prepare for a career, while the system is waiting for you to meet its expectations of your death or jail time? What if you choose to prove them wrong?*

The empty future for too many young people is mirrored in the words of a young inmate named Keith from my summer 2003 workshop at an upstate New York juvenile detention facility:

if only if only

So many times I wanted to cry
but there's something holding me back
I just want to release
some kind of emotion
but no one seems to care
The anger inside me builds
like a thunder's form
An avalanche just engulfing
everyone in sight with the fury
of pain
Now yes now that when
everyone seems to care
because you notice.
It's a shame that you have to see
the bad side
when all I wanted was to be noticed, to be heard,
to have someone to lean on.

Another summer I had a most chilling example of my own premise articulated by a 16-year-old who would soon leave juvenile detention to serve his sentence in a long-term facility. He and his 14-year-old brother decided to sign up for my workshop because they were bored and thought it would better than just hanging out on the unit. They were also told I often brought snacks.

One of the stipulations of my work in this short-term facility was that there was no censorship within the four walls of our classroom. Profanity, discussion of one's case, street monikers, and gang symbols were all forbidden on the incarceration units; however, I had an agreement with the superintendent that there would be complete freedom of speech and thought in workshop. To maintain that freedom, the participants' articulations and utterances had to remain in the room or on paper. If our luxury of open conversation crept back out to the general population, we would lose our rights as poets to speak openly and honestly. We would no longer be able to say what needed to be said without restriction. Freedom of speech was honored, and I believe our relaxed rules were never violated. This, along with the cookies, may have been what brought in new workshop participants.

One Wednesday, in the naïve hope of somehow tapping into a modicum of optimism within the troubled teens in the room, I asked them to imagine their lives in 10 years:

- What did they envision?
- What work did they believe they would be doing?
- Where would they be living and with whom?
- What dreams would they fulfill?

I asked them to describe a day in the life they hoped for in simple detail. All I thought I was asking them to do was to imagine and record those images in a few brainstorming notes. As most of the 12 or so kids sat with their pencils busy at work, one young man raised his hand, indicating that he wanted help. The page was blank. He looked me in the eye. He said, "I can't do this."

"Sure you can."

Again he insisted, "No, I can't."

I rambled through my routine series of probing questions that I can pull out like mittens from my coat pocket. He replied, "Ms., I will probably be dead."

I stopped. There was a stark truth in his words and only one way to respond to his bold, sad statement.

"I can't argue with you. The statistics are not in your favor. But you still have the power to do everything possible to change your life."

I probably told him about poet Jimmy Santiago Baca, actor Charles F. Dutton, or author Nathan McCall, three examples of noted men who had served time, yet chose not to continue on a path that would keep them imprisoned.

One week later, this young man handed in a poem that struck me as evidence of a hidden talent coming forth, the power poetry has to draw beauty from us. It was gorgeous in places with some inventive language, a profound metaphor; it was one of those gems we wait to discover as we teach. I admit that I fussed over it in workshop.

As was the case every summer that I offered the workshop, the young poets' work was to be published in an online poetry Listserv called *PoEmPath*. If the poets produced, they were guaranteed publication. So it happened with this beautiful poem.

A couple of weeks later, the poet was gone, placed in a long-term facility in another part of the state. I told the kids that their poems had been posted on the Internet and I read some of the praise their work received from *PoEmPath* subscribers. As I handed out pencils sharpened for the afternoon's work, one of the girls in the workshop quietly told me that the young man whose work I had applauded had plagiarized his poem. I was stricken. She said he ripped the words from a poem in the liner notes of a CD by Sekou Sundiata, a poet and spoken-word artist whose recordings I had played during one of my visits. He hadn't stolen the whole poem; he took a couple of stanzas and book-ended them with his own words. I was his chump and it saddened me. I had to compose a note for the *PoEmPath* readership to explain that the poem was not new work. I had to confess that a kid got over on me.

About a year later, I received an envelope in my mailbox with an odd return address. Inside I found three folded-up poems, written in blue ballpoint on three-hole-punched notebook paper, simple teen verse, Hip Hop-influenced self-reflections, one about the value of writing a poem. In faint pencil on the outside of the pages, "See. I can do it." And he scrawled his name. I have never heard another word from him and I never did reply, which I regret. I only hope he somehow found a way to value himself and keep himself alive in the process.

I don't know what motivated this young man to write those poems, much less send them to me after all that time. I would like to think that he found something redemptive in creating a poem, in expressing his inner emotions, that language somehow helped him cope with his harsh landscape—both the external and internal.

As I think about the lives of my students, I keep stumbling across little bits of research, information about brain function and language/reading, details about the usage of words, reading comprehension statistics and theories, all sorts of tidbits that occupy countless tiny files in the computer that is my brain. I have heard an estimate that the English language has anywhere from 450,000 to 750,000 words and word forms. Some time ago, I recall hearing that the average American's daily usage of that repository of language is 168 words. This is appalling. Add to that our propensity for abbreviating everything to acronyms and trademarked names and we are pitifully lacking in scope. We have become satisfied with mediocrity when it comes to communication and expression.

The other side of the language factor is that, depending on their socio-economic class, children will have heard somewhere between 350,000 and 3 million words by the time they are registered for kindergarten. These totals represent a huge spread connected to class but still, the data point out that a child is predisposed to language in some form. From Dr. Rudy Crew's remarkable book on school reform in America, *Only Connect: The Way to Save Our Schools*, I found that we agree that there is a direct connection between impoverishment and literacy, as well as academic success. Crew goes further to predict the future economic impact of failing to meet the needs of our nation's children in literacy and education in general.

While reading Sandra Ingerman's *Soul Retrieval: Mending the Fragmented Self through Shamanic Practices*, I pictured face after young face I have taught, portraits of the following:

> Because of today's technology—television programs and movies which don't leave much to the imagination—we have let our ability to imagine become dormant. I think the population that best shows us the extreme of what happens when we lose the ability to imagine and envision is teenagers today. We are actually seeing a group that have lost their souls, and one major reason is that they can't envision either their

personal futures or a bright future for the
planet.

Babies recognize the Golden Arches before they can even talk.[1] Grocery stores have cute shopping carts that look like small cars for toddlers to sit in while parents push through the aisles; others offer toy carts that sport flags proclaiming "Shopper in Training." The language of consumption is everywhere. Most of us are oblivious to how much messaging envelops us daily, imprinting us with desires we may not have developed on our own. We brand our butts, our backs, our feet, and our chests with GAP, Hollister, Nike. In fact, we actually pay big bucks to be walking billboards for internationally known chain stores, musical acts, and tourist traps. We hum the simplistic lyrics of Top-40 rotation, highly sexed-up ditties that negate the years of struggle culminating in civil rights and civil liberties legislation during the 60s and 70s. Nightly we are coerced to ask our doctors for medications with disclaimers longer than the actual television ad copy. We are surrounded by prompts to fulfill our identities as members of a consumer culture, rather than one of creativity.

All the while, our language devolves. Although I too fall prey to lax language, I cringe every time I hear the phrase "her and I went" fall from lips. It is like nails on slate. There are some basics for which many people no longer harbor any worth or pride: spelling, grammar, even penmanship. These are not stressed in ways that compel students to invest their effort and time in learning and displaying quality skills. Additionally, all around them are examples that negate interest or satisfaction in these skills, as opposed to rapid keyboarding. As a species, we were given opposable thumbs. We text. The national fast-food mentality of immediate gratification and the fastest track to receive it is proving to be a critical flaw in our society.

I know poets who often choose not to employ luscious language for fear readers will not know the words. Writers forsake vocabulary when they are in the business of creating worlds, environments, through language. What will we be writing in the future?   Single-syllable word construction of

---

[1] Kopelman, C.A., Roberts, L.M., and Adab P., "Advertising of Food to Children." *Journal of Public Health*, Vol. 29, No. 4, pp. 358-367.

haikus to line bottle tops of the newest beverage sensation? Will brevity be all we are left to employ? We live in a world of acronyms and 140-character messaging. Is it possible that poets can actually be advocates in the quest to avoid linguistic atrophy? The dictionary as a reflection of language itself is ever-changing. We lose words as time passes by failing to use them. Words are deemed antiquated and then relegated to a literary graveyard due to woeful neglect. For instance, each time we listen to the flight attendant as our plane begins to taxi, we are instructed to review the placard in the pocket in front of us and on the wall. Placard is a word that rarely manifests in routine conversational English any longer; it is a word whose only lifeline is provided by the airline industry and it is only in this context that anyone under the age of 21 is likely to have encountered it. Yesterday's "placard" is today's "flier."

We are teaching a generation of students who habitually abbreviate language. I subscribe to a daily e-mail called "A Word a Day" to keep my own skills sharpened. But I am in the business of language and some students will not see how my practice translates to their own lives. Language is power. The dictionary is not a doorstop. It is a weapon as well as a tool. It has the capacity to combat ignorance, deception, and indifference or, at the very least, point them out. Perhaps I will infect at least one student in every class I facilitate with the curiosity to break the inertia and lift that heavy book, open the cover, and check a word simply because it was there, and it was a mystery.

DEMYSTIFYING THE POEM

Georgia A. Popoff

> The point is not to teach—but to evoke, to
> stir our desire to believe differently.
> —Richard Lewis, *When Thought is Young:*
> *Reflections on Teaching and the Poetry of the Child*

How many of you have seen a movie more than twice? How many of you have watched the same movie more than five times? How about more than ten? What is it that makes us rewatch a film, no matter how many times we've seen it before? How many of you were duped on first viewing *The Sixth Sense*, yet saw all the obvious clues the second time around? More important, what did any of you see in the fifth, tenth, thirtieth viewing of your favorite movie that you previously missed? What emotion did you encounter? How did your understanding of that movie change from the first encounter to the most recent?

When a new song hits the popular airwaves, do you, the first-time listener, decipher and understand all of the lyrics by the time that song is over? Probably not. It is more likely that two elements of the song hook you enough to listen a second time: the chorus and the beat. The chorus, by virtue of repetition, creates a sense of comfort and knowingness. The beat is something visceral and compelling. After a few more times listening to the song, the puzzle of the lyric fills in. The bass line or lead guitar, the keyboards or horns become equally recognizable, and we, as audience, acquaint with the song in a fuller sense as all of its parts gather as a whole.

Permit me another line of inquiry. Have you ever returned to an art museum or a gallery specifically to view to a particular piece of art? Is there an art work in your local museum that you visit each time you are there? In all of your occasions to look at art in person, rather than within the pages of a coffee-table book, was the artist there to discuss his or her motivation or the creative process that resulted in that piece being brought into existence? As for that coffee-table book, is there one in your possession that compels you to pick it up time and time again to browse?

As with experiencing a piece of music or visual art, a reader rarely develops a full response to a poem on the basis of a single reading. Any work of art deserves attention and time, repeated visits. Even television shows enjoy rerun seasons and syndication. Why do we think we are expected to consume a poem in a single sitting, much less draw a viable conclusion about its message?

Several years ago while I was preparing to present a workshop for middle- and high-school English teachers, I considered what I truly wanted to communicate as a poet to those who are likely not poets, but who are expected to teach poetry to teenagers. I have spent more than a decade working in schools at every grade level, as well as teaching adult-education classes in reading and creating poetry. I have come to believe that one of the most terrifying questions a teacher can ask of a student of any age is *What does the poem mean?*

It has become very clear to me that this question creates performance anxiety. In fact, I am subject to the same trepidation myself when a poetry workshop is facilitated by a writer who poses that question to prompt critique. I can only imagine what a ninth-grader feels when he is given a W.H. Auden poem to read and is then asked to define the poet's intention on the spot. The frequent disconnect between poet and reader was put another way, very simply, by Phil Memmer, a poet and colleague, during one of his readings in May 2005:

> I always wanted to be a writer, even when I was a kid, but I thought I was going to write fiction. I didn't know that there were living poets until I went to college.

Another thought echoed as I planned my workshop for the teachers. It seems a bit presumptuous to assume we could know what the poem "means," especially since I think we poets often don't fully know what we mean ourselves as we create and recreate a poem, until long after the poem is "finished." We need to step back from the creation, to separate from the act of bringing forth something new into daylight before we fully comprehend the result.

I designed the workshop to introduce the teachers to aspects of a poet's creative process in a way that provided a model for freeing their students to claim a deeper response to poems, rather than drilling on the mechanics and tools of the craft. A reader will never develop a relationship with the content of or draw inference from a poem if the work is approached solely by attempting to decipher some sorcerer's alchemy of literary device, form or structure, and figurative language.

Certainly, curriculum requirements often mandate a timeline with designated units of study. However, attempting to fit poetry into that sort of constraint is antithetical to the nature of the art form and its inherent value. Frequently we discuss the study of a poem as "analyzing" the poem, as if it is a scientific formula, a mathematical equation, or a psychiatric patient on the couch. None of these approaches will help students discern meaning and form a personal relationship with a poem. It is like the difference between reading the engine specs of a Ferrari and taking one for a 100-mph spin on a closed track. One is all in the head; the second is tangible and immediate, solely for the moment and the memory.

When I propose banishing the premise of *analyze this poem*, teachers often respond with audible gasps, then with comments like *That's all very well and good, but we have to prepare students for the state tests. There are things they have to know.*

This is a valid concern, given the current climate of education, but I encourage a different and more comprehensive approach, one that offers a stronger connection between reader and poem, and one that will lead to greater success in facing the gauntlet of standardized testing. This success will be seen in the greater detail and conclusions students reflect after their survey of a poem is complete, as well as the comfort zone students will achieve in their own competency. Think in terms of a five-level process rather than single analysis:

- **Examine**: Read the poem silently, read it out loud to yourself or others, or listen as someone reads it to you. Notice specific details and immerse yourself in the poem multiple times.

- **Experience**: Think about the poem. Try to relate what it says to something you know, have experience with, or have heard about. Continue to notice the details of the poem, the language and word choices, the structure, literary devices, theme, and content.

- **Interpret**: Make connections between what you know from your own life and what the poem is saying. Try to say what the poem has conveyed to you in your own words.

- **Reflect**: Consider all of the elements of the poem and the connections that you have recognized. Ask yourself what there is about the poem that you can imagine or relate to from your own point of view.

- **Respond**: React to what you have found in the poem and create an opinion about it, then share your opinion with someone else.

Whether you are working with students or teachers, rather than asking what the poem *means* perhaps it is more pertinent and productive to investigate *How does the poem make you feel?* Or *What does this poem make you think?* Refine that question to *What do you believe the poet wants you to know, feel, and/or understand from these words?* Follow that question with *What in the poem causes you to think that? How can you say what this poem means to you in your own way? How would you rewrite this poem from your own experience?* Each question addresses content in a different manner, leading the person experiencing the poem into cunning considerations and alleviating the fear of being wrong. By asking readers to identify the clues, the evidence within the language the poet presents to support a theory of meaning that the reader connotes, we are not only able to gauge how a poem comes across. We may also foster a wonderful dialogue of unlimited possibilities based on individuals' different responses to the work.

This difference in understanding is so evident in some ways, but how often does it evade us as readers, teachers, or artists? Do we have the poet before us to fully grasp his intention as we process his piece? Or do the words have to stand independently, with the expectation that they are chosen well enough to bring the audience member or reader to the same conclusion the poet reached in creating the work?

As teachers, we must recognize that a poem will elicit many responses, presenting us with a challenge in quantifying the degree of "correctness" in students' responses. How should a teacher respond to a student's interpretation if it seems too far off the mark from the commonly-accepted interpretation of a poem being studied? What if a student were to suggest that Robert Frost's "Stopping by Woods on a Snowy Evening" is a veiled story of a UFO sighting? If that student could support the premise from evidence in the language of the poem, would that interpretation be incorrect? The point of a poem is to elicit response, not to demand a singular solution for interpretation and understanding. If the reader engages with the content of a poem through her personal history, turning the interpretation a few degrees, there is no harm in permitting that flexibility. Another outcome of multiple and even outlandish interpretations is the discussion that will open among students, a conversation during which they teach each other as they postulate, even debate. That alien sighting in Frost's woods just may provide a phenomenal teachable moment.

The need to be "right" in interpreting the meaning of a poem is a learned behavior that relies on the myth that if you interpret a particular poem in some way other than the accepted or perceived meaning, it means you are just too dumb to "get" poetry. Just days before I presented my teachers' workshop, I articulated this premise to a friend and colleague who is not a poet. She responded that I had found words for the reason she is terrified of reading poetry. I believe my friend is in the company of many. I understand the terror completely. I often have the same concern, even though I am a poet myself. I need time to be with a poem, alone within my imagination, so I can examine it as often as I will listen to a song or watch the same movie, each time digging deeper into what the poem evokes for me in both feeling and understanding. I certainly do not find all I need to know in one reading or listening.

Sometimes I do not even comprehend the "meaning" of my own poems to their fullest extent, particularly in the early stages of the life of a poem. It is like some foreign language that I need to leave alone for a few days while I cultivate a personal translation. This is an intuitive journey at best. There have been times when someone who has read one of my poems gave me a perspective that deepened my own understanding. Sometimes these sage readers are students. I was delighted to read Richard Hugo's "confession" regarding a poem that he cited in his book, *The Triggering Town*. He stated that he did not really know what he had meant in a poem written when he was a younger poet; he just appreciated the sound and sensibility of the poem. He is quite certain that he knew what he meant when he wrote it, but although he no longer felt confident about his intended meaning he was quite taken with the poem's musicality, and that was enough for him.

What relief! What an opportunity to teach from a different axis! The vehicle to achieve the nuance and emotion is the metaphor, which is, in turn, supported by all of the tools at hand for the poet. These tools are the elements that are required curricula for the teacher who has to complete the "poetry unit" at some point during the school year. This analytical process is even more difficult for the elementary-school teacher, for whom there are many core content areas to cover and perhaps poetry is not a strong suit or interest.

Once I began teaching poetry from this more expansive perspective, I found that I had a way to help both classroom teachers and students. It is important to remember that a poem is first and foremost a creative work of art, not an equation. Poets, as artists, give themselves over to something bewitching and inexplicable. Each achieves a poem by different methods. Some are quite disciplined, others more driven by the moment of inspiration. However, few sit down to build a poem the way folks once built Sears houses. There is something else happening, a kind of "zone" that brings forth a draft poem, followed by a revision process. In other words, it is part magic and part sweat equity.

It is necessary to explain these concerns in ordinary metaphor, which is why I began with the series of questions about film, music, and visual art. Students frequently view movies over and over, especially in this age of DVD and Blu-ray. Until prompted, they may not even be conscious that they see new things in the background of scenes or understand the plot and all of its twists more readily after multiple viewings. Once students understand how they engage with other forms of art, the value of working their way organically through a poem becomes clearer to them.

A reader will never love all poets or all poems. There is a subjectivity and preference in this, as in all art forms. You will never all love the same movies, you will never agree on which painter is the best, some of you like opera and others Clint Black or Kanye West. But there is a poem for everyone and there is a more liberating way to enter the poem so you and your students will be able to claim it as your own.

ONE BAG EMPTY

∎

Georgia A. Popoff & Quraysh Ali Lansana

> For too long, poets have been like the
> members of the ancient cult of Magi—
> investing the simplest rituals and concepts
> with mists and taboos.
>
> Anyone can learn to write poetry.
> Individually, the techniques are simple,
> though it takes concentration to learn
> them—concentration and practice. No one
> can teach someone to write great poetry,
> however. Only God or the Muses give
> talent—all the teacher can give is
> knowledge.
>   —Lewis Turco, *Poetry: An Introduction*
>   *through Writing*

Creative writing is not often linear and it is certainly a complex endeavor. As writers, we must create a consistent discipline of allowing time to write, during which we may stumble into inspiration. We must train our minds to receive that lightning bolt, but discipline aids inspiration by establishing fertile ground in which to root. Once germination has occurred, the hard work of many drafts and revisions leads to the final result of a poem. The poet must also remain immersed in the work of other poets, the lineage, in order to forge her own place and capacity, just as John Coltrane was able to break tradition and change the face of jazz by knowing its history, the history of music itself, so well that he created something completely avant-garde and exhilarating.

In the writing process, a poet may start with a particular idea or theme and, somewhere along the journey, be hijacked. We are open to discovery and through that openness we find greater success than if we simply filled in the blanks of acrostics of our names. The non-linear aspects of creating a poem—including abstraction, metaphor, and atypical syntax—often instill hesitancy among student writers, a fear that they haven't the skill required to be successful. We must demonstrate that poets are not magically different, that poets have to strive to attain a final product. A poet does not just sit before the page, pen in hand or finger to keyboard, blindly practicing automatic writing from some ephemeral source. The mystique is in one inspiring moment; then comes the work of composing the poetic music. The first draft is a launch point, not a final destination. When students understand this, they may more willingly work to connect with a poem. They may also be more willing to revise and strive for better writing themselves.

When we plan a vacation to a place we have never been, we are eager and ready to immerse in every aspect of that new environment. The key to successful travel is in the luggage we select and what we carry on the sojourn. A poem is much like travel. Through careful reading, one can immerse in the environment a poem creates. Therefore, sharing poetry with students invites them to enter new worlds. In addition, we must remember to travel with one bag empty, ready to fill with our "souvenirs," the awareness and understanding we derive from the poem. If we are open to interacting within the poet's metaphoric world, there will be great discoveries and we will be enriched, perhaps better prepared to see, listen, and appreciate our own environments more readily and fully.

Just as we cannot fully comprehend all of the nuances of another culture in one week-long excursion, we must revisit a poem repeatedly, reading each word carefully, noting the relationships among them, the deliberate language choices the poet has made, as carefully as we notice landmarks of the geography in which we are tourists.

There are two ways to map the journey through a poem: reading the words on the page and listening to the words take flight, full of breath, as they are read aloud. Each of these maps provides a perspective with which to interpret the landscape. By referring to these maps repeatedly, the reader/listener becomes more familiar with and more confident in her understanding of the route and how soon she will arrive at her destination: comprehension.

Compare the structure of a poem to fishing, with three key components matching three phases of angling for trout. The title of the poem is the bait that attracts the reader as he flips through a collection of poems, or that catches the attention of the listener in an audience. The first line becomes the hook that secures the fish by the jaw. The dance begins as the body of the poem unfolds in a way similar to the choreography between fish and angler. The fish may struggle, but the fisherman hopes to succeed in keeping him on the line. The last line of the poem is the net, pulling the trophy into the boat or onto shore. A memorable last line—one that is not overly clever or that does not sum up the poem with the implication that the reader will not understand without explanation—will rest in the reader's memory for a long time.

Let us go to dry land and another metaphor: The title is the contextual anchor or oasis if one gets stranded in the poem. Should you lose your way in that vast desert of *I don't get it* that so many readers slog through, the title will offer the relief of reminder, a confirmation regarding poetic theme and its companion, emotion.

Although it is common practice, approaching a poem as a formula to be analyzed and deconstructed drains the poem of its power. To examine a poem simply through the literary devices it employs and the descriptive language it includes does not create a reliable methodology from which to draw deep inference or to connect with the inspiration and intention of the poet. Poetry offers more than literary gymnastics; in fact, the devices employed by the poet are elements of advancing the poem's message and emotional substance, and affording the reader an extraordinary vision. Literary devices are not the content; they are a part of the mechanics that support the vehicle. In the best of practices the form becomes translucent, revealing ideas, images, and impact. Encourage students to unpack a poem like a suitcase full of travel mementos, to open it and take out each piece, to reflect and remember, to daydream and ground, to grow and soar.

It used to be that the teacher who spent the school year instructing, observing, and fostering each child's development was viewed as most capable of assessing student achievement. Now standardized tests rule and teachers are expected to prepare students to provide the "right" answers about a poem's meaning.

How much more valuable it is to use poetry to teach critical-thinking strategies that stretch beyond the poem. The layered approach of multiple readings, listening to the words, questioning vocabulary, identifying literary mechanisms, recognizing the musicality, and then interpreting the metaphoric and imagistic expression is a far different angle than *analyze this poem*. It is an approach that is active, comprehensive, and stimulating. Ideally, this approach also presents a platform for the creation of student work and guideposts to writing effective, imaginative verse that will serve as a "speaker's box" for students to communicate their perceived place in our world.

STRETCHING EXERCISES

▦

Quraysh Ali Lansana

Sometime during the spring of 1998, I had the opportunity to participate in a poetry workshop conducted by National Book Award winner Reginald Gibbons. Gibbons and I had interacted for some time at that point, as we were both intimately involved with Guild Complex, a noted non-profit literary center birthed at Guild Books, a progressive bookstore that, unfortunately, is no longer in existence. The Guild Complex remains one of the Midwest's premier literary centers. Though Gibbons was always kind and respectful, I was a young poet with no formal training, intimidated by his pedigree and, truth be told, slow to trust an established White male.

Many of the ideas presented by Gibbons involved approaches to craft, especially deconstructing and rethinking linear structure in language and line. Reg shared two simple ideas that indelibly impacted *southside rain*, my first book of poetry, as well as my teaching philosophy.

I consider myself a direct descendant of the Black Arts Movement poets, more so contextually than aesthetically. A few months before the workshop I left the funky wordsmyths, a four-year-old poetry band on the brink of national exposure, anchored by Oscar "Bobo" Brown III. The youngest son of the world-renowned singer/songwriter Oscar Brown Jr., Bobo was an incredible musician and vocalist. The wordsmyths performed "hard-hitting' poetry and music" almost every other day for years. Keith Kelley, the other primary poet, and I crafted Black-focused, politically-charged language on an ever-changing landscape of blues, jazz, gospel, and, of course, funk. My work was rooted in the influence of Haki Madhubuti, Lucille Clifton, and Gwendolyn Brooks, and was constructed to be read aloud, though I've never employed "slam-poet" aesthetics, and loathe the term "performance poet."

Reg dropped a bomb on my poetry sensibilities at the time. *Instead of placing the "pay-off line" at the poem's close, why not put it at the beginning or in the center, then work to and from that line?* The pay-off line in this context is the answer to the poem's question, the idea that sews up all the seams. It seems simple enough, yet many poets, established or emerging, continue to work within the paradigm of ending a poem with "the answer." This opened up a new world for me.

Gibbons' other jewel of advice focused on the notion of poet as athlete. "Athletes stretch," he said. "Poets should stretch, too. We should present ourselves aesthetic hurdles to jump over or obstacles to move around." Faced with these challenges, it is incumbent on us to devise strategies and inroads to overcome or negotiate the obstacles, all in service to the poem. This led me to a new appreciation of traditional forms. Crafting a sonnet or sestina, which I would not have considered before Gibbons' workshop, now was a challenge requiring the use of dormant muscles. Once flexed, those muscles needed more expansive, demanding, and consistent exercise. I felt poetically healthier after work outside my normal routine.

Forms, including Afaa Michael Weaver's "bop" and the "kwansaba," created by Eugene Redmond, are now components of my syllabi. As all knowledge is intended to function, I have internalized Reg's "poet-as-athlete" construct and created my own entrance ramp via jazz music innovators Miles Davis and John Coltrane. Miles and Trane studied as many different musical traditions as they could find before beautifully abusing the music in the ways they did. They entrenched themselves in the possibilities presented by cultures far and wide, then developed new possibilities that asked questions of what we think we know (listen to "Kind of Blue" or "A Love Supreme" to hear and feel this questioning). This is what all teachers ask of their students.

Teaching poetry with first-year drama division students at The Julliard School afforded me an opportunity to play with language utilizing methods we don't often employ in writing classes. However, I found a way to adapt the "poet-as-athlete" idea during two amazing years at the famed performing-arts school.

I asked students to leave the building and go out on the streets of Manhattan's Upper West Side, find a spot, and people watch. They were then to wait and watch for an unsuspecting stranger whose appearance, disposition, and energy caught their attention, for whatever reasons. I instructed them to follow this person for a few minutes, from a safe distance, of course. While following their "subjects" they had to quickly internalize and mimic their physical movements, their rhythms and vibrations, and jot down what they perceived to be their stories. The next week, the students had to perform both the non-verbal and spoken internal dialogues of their chosen strangers.

Later in the semester, after tracking strengths and weaknesses of each student, I assigned every student to find a specific poem or theatrical monologue that forced them to reach outside usual tropes. For example, the messy hipster young woman had to find her footing in *Pollyanna*. One of the more compelling teaching moments in my career occurred when I witnessed a young Midwestern White man, who was sheltered from ethnic diversity until moving to New York City, interpret the most strident language of Malcolm X· He was shaken to the core, and to tears. He was forever changed as an actor, as he told me. I had done my job.

The "poet-as-athlete" concept is applicable to K-12 instruction with a variety of twists. One is to on focus on form by imposing a specific line length, word count, and/or number of stanzas as the hurdles to glide over, while avoiding the standard traditional poetic forms of cinquain, diamonte, acrostic, or concrete poems, which are relied upon too often. Ask students to omit personal pronouns, articles, conjunctions, so the language relies more on image and idea, as well as active verbs to deliver the poem's thematic thread. Another approach is to assign several key words that must appear in the poem with the goal of finding as many different contexts as possible for those words, thus strengthening vocabulary skills along with creative talents. Teachers can look to their scope and sequence for relevant curriculum tie-ins to incorporate into their lesson plans. Particular literary devices may be employed to embellish the word-puzzle assignment.

I push. I vigorously encourage students to think and write outside their normal Skinner boxes. I challenge them to investigate every nook and cranny, every angle. I teach not as final answer, but as seasoned response.

I've grown considerably since Gibbons' workshop. Reg has remained a guide and mentor for me as both poet and human. I am grateful that he didn't give up on me when, like many youngsters, I possessed the fool-hearted belief I knew it all. Many of us have encountered young poets who don't read poetry or revise their work because they consider influence and change to be negatives. They are no different from the many seasoned poets who have, due to success, written essentially the same poem for five books. All of us benefit from a solid work-out plan.

Keep It Simple, Poet

Deliberation and Economy of Language

Georgia A. Popoff

an you tell your story in six words? This is the gauntlet thrown, and just like potato chips, once you start composing "six-word memoirs" you can't stop. They become habitual. The rhythm is so natural to our daily speech patterns that you won't even realize until after the words are spoken that you are constantly thinking in six-word cycles.

When I was introduced to *Six-Word Memoirs*—an anthology series from *SMITH Magazine*—it took some time before I fell into stride with the form. Then I was hooked, especially for using the concept in my teaching. Attributed to a challenge issued to Ernest Hemingway to write a short story in six words, this form has developed almost a cult following. Six words! Anyone can write that much and feel successful. Daily, people are choosing six words that best describe who they are and their life status, then posting them to the *SMITH Magazine* website, another of those social networks that flood the Internet these days, but this one is allocated to these short self-reflections. The best part is that immediately, much in the same way Facebook and Twitter feed on our need to be heard, the statement of being is posted up on the site. (Since sometimes there is an issue with content and language not being appropriate for all ages, there is now a site specifically for teens in addition to the adults-only website.)

But let's talk about the application in class. Young people may not always think about the different faces we all present to the world daily. When we ask students to state who they are, right in the moment, in six words, they begin a process of both self-examination and creative writing. There is no need for complicated narrative, not even complete sentences— just six words to describe a mood or a belief about self. There is very little resistance to such a simple assignment.

I find the best way to start is by sharing a few examples from a *Six-Word Memoir* anthology or website so an expectation is communicated, a model is provided. After asking students to write about themselves at that moment, in six words, I move on to engaging the class in a discussion about changeable identity. A series of questions gets us rolling:

- Are you the same person in class that you are at home with your parents?

- Do you act the same way when you are at the mall or on the ball court with your friends as you do when you visit your grandparents?

- Are you the same on the bus ride home as you are in your church, synagogue, or mosque?

As we invite young people to broaden their awareness of the world around them and the place they occupy in the whole, the magic starts to brew. It becomes easy to prompt more responses to questions such as:

- Who were you at 7:00 AM?

- Who will you be at 3:00 PM?

- Who were you last night in that very last moment before you fell asleep?

- Who were you on the first day of kindergarten?

- Who will you be when you graduate from high school?

- What was the biggest risk you ever took?

- What is your biggest fear?

Each question can be answered simply, in only six words, and once the pattern is established students respond quickly and enjoy sharing their work with classmates. Ideally, the responses from peers encourage them to strive for the best adjectives, the conscious selection of words that will say the most in a short span.

I discover beautiful pearls in these responses. A young lady in a rural community creates "African soul in a White body." The young man who is slow to start writes, "I feel like mud here today." Another teen describes risk in "I talked back to my father." When I asked, "How did that work for you?" his simple response was expected. "Not so well." The statements are sometimes mundane, sometimes poignant. There are hopes for the future, expectations of what will come.

Then there are windows into the events and dramas of young lives, some of which are more challenging than anything many adults face. One spring, during the course of a two-week high-school residency, I was scheduled for a single-class visit. The tenth-grade literacy class was industrious as students met each of my prompts. They eagerly shared their writing, each student learning more about the others as the snapshots of their lives were spoken into the air. The bell rang and the flow towards the door was instantaneous, except for one boy who did not budge. Handsome and quiet, a sturdy, muscular young man, he had not chosen to read his work aloud. I walked over and asked if I could read what he had created and he quietly agreed.

For several weeks, this student had been withdrawn and sullen, very unlike his usual demeanor, to the point that his teachers were wondering about the change in his behavior. His words provided their answer. On the page, in troubled pencil marks, he had written six or seven short statements, including "Her parents, my parents, me Dad." "Her stomach's growing. I'm not concerned." "She's throwing up. I'm sick inside." His girlfriend was pregnant and life was going to change. I did not have a relationship with this student, so I offered a few words of understanding as his teacher approached. I excused myself as she began her counsel.

After students became familiar with the six-word memoir, the next step was to make this exercise relate to the bigger lesson of crafting a poem and communicating effectively. I determined that the six-word lines would be a terrific starting point for stanzas. Student writers would have already found something to write about that was within their own scope of reference. I asked them to add a few lines after each six-word memoir, assigning additional conditions such as literary devices and specific stanza lengths. This gave the writers a chance to grow beyond the tight word count. They could readily create a relevant, autobiographical poem with competence. Since so many students need some structure or organizing principle for their thoughts, this was a terrific mechanism for enabling them to move forward with confidence.

The six-word memoir or the structured form I then devised does not work only with teenagers. This structure has also been successful with much younger students. I offered an in-service workshop to a group of teachers from different grade levels in which I presented the process as one of the varied activities I shared. I was delighted to walk into a first-grade classroom of one of the participants several weeks later to find a gorgeous bulletin-board display of memoirs, all hanging like laundry on the clothesline with bright illustrations of each student's unique vision. What a lovely surprise.

Another approach I've used with success is to ask students to consider that many of us feel one way on the inside but project a different self to the world. When I first considered this concept as a platform for creating poems, it was based on a lesson shared by a teacher colleague, developed during her many years of teaching middle school. I adapted her theme to use in my own work, with much gratitude for the inspiration. All of us have to maintain a front at one point or another in life. It may just be that we feel sad and have to go to work. It may be that we feel misunderstood by others. We may be very shy and maneuvering through life has caused us to develop an outer shell, a way to cope. This inside/outside awareness is another construct that leads to success in generating poetry, once the conversation with the class has illustrated the intention of the lesson.

As I tried the inside/outside prompts, I began by asking students to close their eyes as I placed something in their hands, that "thing" being an orange. I wanted them to describe the outside of the object without visual reference. We discovered that the skin of an orange may feel like a basketball, a snake, a football, or rubber, to name a few connections. We discussed the inside of an orange, that the whole is comprised of segments. The outside is resistant and sturdy, the inside is soft and juicy. We talked about the varied tastes associated with an orange as well; although the pulp and juice are sweet, the rind and those annoying strings that cling to the fruit when we peel it are bitter.

I projected images of trees, images of tree roots, and rings of trees cut crosswise on the interactive white board. The point was simple. What we generally relate to as "tree" is much less than the whole. I was reminded of the old adage of the blind men trying to identify an elephant while each of them felt a different part of the animal.

After that, I pulled up some images of Romare Bearden's artwork from the Internet without any set up. I asked what the students saw, what they believed they knew about the artist from looking at the work. Invariably, they recognized the images of African-American life, they understood the cultural references and had much to say about the colors, the patterns, the themes.

I then posted a photo of Bearden, with his light-hued skin, his flat nose, his terrific hat and shining eyes. I asked them what they thought they knew about this man on the screen. Hands raised to offer answers; as I called on different students, I received varied responses. This was a man who was German, he was Polish, he was old, he looked happy, he was smart.

Imagine the disbelief when I told them that this was the artist who had created all those colorful collages and paintings we had looked at previously. Echoes of "No way!" and "What?! How could that be?" swirled through the room. One student exclaimed, "He's a racist!" Now that was a stretch for me, so I asked why he thought that. Based on the images that this young man had seen in the artwork, and on his assumption that Bearden was White, he felt them cartoonish and he interpreted the work as derogatory.

We took the time to discuss the sad history of segregation, the difficult choices light-skinned people of African descent sometimes made to "pass," the threat Bearden's light skin posed to his parents in the deep south of the early 20th Century, and this remarkable artist's election to chronicle Black life.

Then I presented the following simple template:

On the outside, I am _____.
On the inside, I am _____.

I asked the students to create at least five pairs of statements. After they completed that assignment, I asked them to expand on their thoughts by creating similes that would incorporate adjectives and adverbs, for example:

On the outside, I am (adjective) like a (adjective) (noun).

On the inside, I am as (adverb) as a (adjective) (noun).

The final result would be 10-line poems that tell readers the story of how these students navigate their interior realms as they move through the outer reality and all of its pressures, expectations, and quick glances. Again, there was enough structure for those who need an order to follow, but there was plenty of room for expansion and personal adaptation for those who were ready to expound upon their responses.

The most touching series of both six-word-memoir and inside/outside poems were created by high-school freshmen who were members of a self-contained classroom. The students were mostly young people who have been diagnosed with conditions on the autism spectrum. Their poignant articulation of the divergence between their interior selves and the outer was remarkable. Here is one example:

> On the outside I am absolute like an adequate soldier.
> On the inside I am calm, like an agile octopus.
> On the outside I am as amiable as a cub.
> On the inside I am as troublesome as the devil.
> On the outside I am cockeyed like an oblivious octopus that is blind.
> On the inside I am open like a permanent ocean.
> On the outside I am as poised as a professor who just got fired.
> On the inside I am as fresh as pickle relish.

The succinct truths of their short life stories were touching. In all instances, they maintained excellent humor in their reflections. They were comfortable in their differences and extremely supportive of each other. They knew each other well and could easily call out attributes of the others as we talked about adjectives. Their community of eight could have been a model for all communities. They tolerated each other's foibles. They celebrated each other's creativity. They liked each other and they liked words. We got along famously and I am ever touched by their poems and the friendship they extended over the course of my week in their classroom.

Gadgets, Games, and Media Literacy

Georgia A. Popoff & Quraysh Ali Lansana

An Internet search for "digital natives" reveals a new term to identify young people for whom computers and video games are as common in their lives as Cheerios and backpacks. School-aged children are so comfortable with digital media that those of us who came up between the Baby Boom of the 1950s and the 80s' Hip-Hop explosion are often awed and confounded by the natural ease and skill as small fingers fly over keypads or find games hidden on our cell phones. Not only are children fearless when approaching a new computer, video-game system, or "smart phone," but they also have been inundated with media images since birth, branding them as consumers. We are all moving at warp speed and patience is seemingly and hopelessly outmoded.

The classroom has changed considerably with the advent of the computer age and, particularly, the expansive growth of the Internet over the past 15 years. Blackboards are often secondary to interactive Whiteboards with multimedia capability. PowerPoint slide shows often replace poster-board projects with stenciled letters and globs of glitter. Research may start at a computer terminal in the school media center, formerly the library, rather than the card catalogue. Also missing are flash cards and felt charts for learning ones, tens, hundreds; now the screen in the front of the class flashes animated numerals with clever soundtracks. The privilege of erasing the blackboard or the enthusiastic clapping of erasers, both dusting fingers and nostrils with chalk, are now replaced with the opportunity to calibrate the Whiteboard screen by pressing the hatch marks in the corners and center, with the accompanying arcade blips that sound through the room. Everything is either glitzy or formulaic, perhaps resulting in much less for kids to imagine for themselves.

There are numerous advantages to all of these resources. We have the ability to search synonyms on www.thesaurus.com while the whole class debates the best word choice for a collaboratively composed poem; everyone "on the same page," as it were. We can immediately respond to classroom discussion about art and history by pulling up the homepage of the Romare Bearden Foundation, leading to a conversation about acceptance and the notion of "passing" during the dark times of profound and overt segregation. We can listen to the sound of the owl referenced in a story or poem. We can find facts with ease when asked questions we cannot answer.

Educators can also prepare a lesson-plan format as a template. As we move through each class period, we can note specific comments, then save the responses from each class as separate files that become delightful and timely forms of documentation. The times are nearly extinct when, at the end of a class, the eraser eliminated that small piece of teaching history to make way for the next lesson. If the interactive tool is not available, then we can use our digital cameras or even our cell phones to capture notes for later. This is a tremendous opportunity for those of us responsible not just for the teachable moment, but also for assessment, accountability, and redesign of our lessons at a future date.

The downsides also exist: the faulty connections, the teaching artist who has never encountered a new tool but must learn how to use it on the fly or fly solo, the teacher who is reluctant to embrace technology, blocks on websites imposed by district policies, and, again, the loss of active imagination. Additionally, in implementing a lesson plan, we may be challenged if we rely too much on a computer. Some districts have such limited funds that the number of computers available in the classroom or the whole school may prevent achieving the intended final product, such as a promised anthology of student work. We must also remember that prevalent as a computer may be in a typical American home, there are still many homes that are PC-free zones, due to income, socio-economic class, or even something as simple as limited Internet and cable access in some geographic areas.

Some districts are investing in small public-address systems for the classroom so both teachers and students can speak into microphones, rather than students learning how to project well enough to be heard on the other side of the room, or for the teacher to enforce the need to be quiet and attentive when someone else is speaking.

There is heated debate regarding this "information age" and the toys available to us while teaching. Some find fault with Whiteboard technology. Some think we cannot live without it. As with any innovation in technology, there will be pros and cons, proponents and nay-sayers. Technology brings many benefits to the process of teaching, but there is still something to be said for the simple lesson that relies solely on imagination.

Recently the news flashed a quick item about Japanese robots programmed to deliver standard classroom lessons. The automated age has gone beyond the factory to schools. But where is the ability of that machine to see the spark in a child's eye, or the confusion; if the lesson is either compelling or confounding? Can a machine do anything comparable to the teacher, other than rote lessons and roll call? How does one program a robot for classroom management? What if a child just needs a few moments of guidance and encouragement, or asks an abstract question?

Consider the third-grader who has just witnessed a butterfly emerge from the cocoon that his class has watched for weeks. He pounds his forehead with his palm, exclaiming, "I just don't get it! How does that happen?!" This boy understands that the caterpillar wraps itself in a pouch of fine silk, curled like a cashew. He has learned that the caterpillar dissolves into liquid. But who among us, including 8-year-olds, mannequins that can talk, or even biologists, can actually say how that liquid reorganizes into a Monarch butterfly? That is the place where magic and the unanswerable upstage our logical brains, the place where poetry may be born.

The old adage is sage: every picture is worth a thousand words. When a student is asked to illustrate what she sees on the video screen deep in her brain while she listens to a poem, there is already a frame of reference, a connection that transcends language. Drawing the poem works just as well in an adult poetry workshop as it does with a class of first-graders or middle-school kids. Image moves beyond language. Say *table* and most of us agree what that object will look like. Images drive us and they define us.

Through visual imagery, classes of English language learners have a common point for communication and creativity. Ask a student to display a picture she has drawn of her favorite food and listen for the choral response: "Pizza!" Or direct a group of "tween" boys at summer camp to draw their own stories after a guided tour through the uncharted planet hiding in the woods that they have just visited as astronauts. All the spaceships blasting across sheets of construction paper have separate stories. One red dot on the dashboard of a space pod is more than a crayon mark. It is an adventure that results in pushing the emergency button, releasing the freeze ray that stops all the dangerous alien ships advancing on our weary young space captain who saves the day, perhaps Earth itself. There is a full narrative inside his head. He knows every detail, which can be harnessed in pictures and then the words may follow.

t is likely that familiar symbols from television, DVDs, video games will also appear. Pokémon shows up throughout the elementary school; high-school students draw Animé as they listen in class. This common iconography cannot be escaped, any more than the second-grade notion of *tree*, which often includes a hole in the middle of an obviously deciduous tree with a red bird perched on a jutting brown branch. Where else would the nest be after all? That artist may live in rural Wisconsin, Phoenix, the Bronx, southern California, but *tree* is a hiding place for squirrels and birds, capped with a big green cloud of leaves. These imprints allow us to agree on so many commonalities. To push beyond the expected visual icon is the more profound work of encouraging students to create poetry. When we press our classes to be scribes for their own creative images, the air fills with chatter and excitement, once we get past the groans. *Aaawwww...we've got to write?!*

Let's examine this poem by Janine Simon, a young woman from New York City, included in Scholastic's *Best Teen Writing of 2006:*

Purpose

It's hard to write what I mean
　　　　　And mean what I say
About who I am as of today.
　　　　　The vulnerability of being *me*.

I'm on the verge of illiteracy.
　　　　I can't describe who I be.

73

I get stumped when I try
          to create a metaphor
That represents what my existence is for
        Deliver it with creativity
Make it sound raw.

It's even harder to explain why
I perm, press, and brush my hair back
Until
          It's deemed desirable, smooth and flat.
But I cringe with disgust at the sight of that
       Infamous natural nap.
       "What's wrong with that?"
They say it's wack to be black
When she taunts
"That chick is black till she's blue"
         Yo sis, what are you?
This manipulative modern day media is a tool
That hammered drilled locked and screwed
My creative thinking into a box
Labeled Sony, Panasonic, or Sharp
Through which subliminal hypnotism
By the American system
Drowns my psyche with dominant ideologies
Dictating what my appearance should be.

Flashy commercials bait hook and reel me in
Selling cellular phones shiny and chrome;
iPods, expensive jeans with topless broads in them
Clothes European cut so I can't fit them.
Swirling in this cyclone and twilight zone
Of conformity and clones

But wait—
There's a voice inside screaming:

> Save your soul
> > Just pick up the pen
> > > And put down the remote control.

In her poem, Janine questions everything about identity and her desire to wear a certain pair of jeans, how to style her hair, whether to stick earbuds in her head as she travels to school. This is a person conscious of logos and how the symbols of advertising direct her as she navigates her environment; a poet who recognizes that many of us negotiate through a stupor of images imposed by Madison Avenue, which funded brain research and studies in psychology to get a better hold on how to sell product. She is very conscious of her cultural identity and all of those messages buried like cookies on websites beneath the surface of FUBU, Phat Farm, and Afro Sheen, much less *Cosmopolitan*, *Essence*, and the Miss America Pageant.

In the 21st Century, we live in front of screens. Students walk through the halls with cords hanging from their ears and moms walk through supermarkets with Bluetooth plugs hiding under their hair. We are media savvy and we are urgent to have everything at our fingertips. Text language mirrors the written lyrics of a Prince song. What happens when we ask a class of eighth-graders to translate a poem by Langston Hughes into cell-phone text notation? It takes a different shape, and suddenly heads are bent toward the desk again, puzzling and producing. It is possible to bridge the generational differences in this manner while still accessing Hughes' original intent of language and meaning.

As we read a screen, the scroll allows us to scan rather than absorb. Our eyes are stilled as the waterfall of words and advertisements flows upward and disappears behind the tool bars. Will we become a wiki world of snippets and clips, in which we are jacks of all trades, masters of none? Would the book suffer as dearly as the electronic device when dropped in a sand dune?

Students must be prepared for digital input and response. They need keyboarding skills, they need to be adept at surfing through the unlimited confusion of resources we call the Internet. And they certainly need to know how to download the newest Eminem ringtone if they are going to have a social life. Their parents will count on them to troubleshoot the computer that may drive not only the family QuickBooks program, but also the newest version of *Grand Theft Auto*. They will need computer skills to work at Walmart or to apply to MIT. We are in the midst of automated everything. A student will likely prefer to read a poem on the screen and then write his own so he can see the words stretch across the white document layered over his Facebook profile, his e-mail inbox, and his iTunes library window.

Jesters, Avatars, and Layered Language

Poems as Video Games

Georgia A. Popoff

Teaching is a performance art in which we are actors on an ever-changing stage, working from a constantly revised script. Improvisation is a remarkable tool, as well as a prerequisite for success. One spring day as I strove to connect with some middle-school students distracted by the season, I discovered a suitable and engaging metaphor to encourage the class to read a poem repeatedly. Suddenly, as if I were a ventriloquist's dummy, my mouth spoke words that have changed my approach entirely since that day: *Think of a poem as a new video game you just brought home from the game store.*

This was a keeper. I initiated the challenge: *Let's see how many levels we can achieve.* I would be very liberal in awarding advancement, each level further encouragement to continue. I had to think on my feet as we worked through the poem I chose for the lesson. Hands jutted into the air to signal a possible answer. There was much discussion, and we were drawing many more individual responses and conclusions than we had been 40 minutes earlier. I was hopping around the front of the room like a jester, guiding the class further and further into inference. They hardly knew they were learning.

Over the summer I parsed out the premise with tremendous anticipation for my upcoming school year. It was likely I would receive a level of buy-in that would be refreshing and I knew I could adapt the premise for most grade levels. I was confident because I had a connection point that made sense given the comfort zone of digital-age students. All I needed was a good poem and a group of kids who trusted my prompts, and they could be rock stars!

Fall arrived, new students; let's start it off. In the early days of my practice, I realized that the elementary-school age group affords the most opportunity to create an imaginative play space within the confines of the classroom. There are fewer points of resistance to play; those become more evident in the middle- and high-school years. After the host teacher introduces me, I provide a bit of personal background, such as where I live, when I started writing poetry, that I am a poet because I love both reading and writing words.

Then I circle the room, meeting each student, extending my hand as I say, *Hi, I am Ms. Popoff. It is good to meet you...Good morning, Ms. Popoff...What is your name?* I shake each student's hand, waiting to hear their names in return. If I am unsure of pronunciation or need to hear the name again, I may also ask the student to spell it for me. This not only helps me remember, but also lets the students know I respect them as individuals and want to learn something important about them. We are our names and acknowledging students by name is vital to success.

I return to the front of the room. *So here is the deal: when you shook my hand you did not know it at the time, but you just became a part of my video game.* The kids search for joysticks, computer terminals, anything familiar. I explain further: *We are a virtual video game, right here in this room. We are the game and each of you is an avatar. I am the Game Master. I make the rules and I have the power of moving you through the levels. Our game is called "Poetry Detectives" and each of you is now a detective in the quest. Now who can tell me what a detective does?*

My task is to guide students to examine the poem's clues so carefully that the mysteries of context and meaning are solved. *Okay, another thing about shaking my hand: that is Level One. You have already achieved the first level of the game so you now get your first piece of important equipment. As I shook your hands, I placed on your desks your Official, Imaginary, Invisible Poetry Detective Thinking Caps. Take a look. Do you see yours? Please put your thinking caps on and we will go to the next level.*

Astoundingly, it works! Now we are in a world of our own design. Nothing matters on the other side of the classroom door. Some children describe their caps. They are elaborate and wonderful. Some children want to fold paper into hats, they want something tangible. Some are reluctant and think the rest of us are nuts, but we usually drag them along into fantasy. Others are concerned that they will forget, lose, or leave their hats at home and will not have them tomorrow. Well, there is a very easy fix for that! They are imaginary. We can always imagine our replacement for a lost thinking cap, or we can imagine a way to transport a hat from the place it was last seen to where we are right now. [**Note:** Teachers may choose to have the children make actual hats and badges but I leave it to the children's imaginations in the interests of both time and, more important, creative process.]

I also generally point out that the teacher whose class I am visiting is the Assistant Game Master, thus involving the teacher in our process and not negating his authority. The teacher becomes the Game Master when I am not present, establishing a process that can continue after I am gone, both for the rest of the day and throughout the school year.

It is easy to achieve Level Two. Read the poem silently, to yourself, two times. The quiet is palpable. As I scan the room, I also conduct a preliminary assessment of reading skills based on the time it takes individuals to complete the task. I notice which students are quick readers and those who require more time, and I will watch to see if these first observations become patterns. Once the class has read the poem twice, they earn the second important piece of equipment for any investigator of language, their *Official, Imaginary, Invisible Poetry Detective Badge.* I ask them all to pin their badges on and we advance through the next levels of inquiry to unfold the meaning of the poem. We start keeping a tally of our levels of achievement on the board.

Next we hear the poem aloud several times, read by different students. I tell them about the days before humans could read and write; just as it takes each of us time to learn how to do these things, humans had to develop those abilities over time. I talk to them about the days before books, when our stories had to be told and retold orally, when news passed from one village to another, delivered by voice. Rhyme and rhythm were the mechanisms that helped storytellers remember facts, details, and timelines. I celebrate poetry's two delivery methods—written and oral—and note that each time we hear the poem in a different voice, we hear it differently and discover new clues to its meaning.

If the class gets too rowdy, I have also figured out that I have a new tool to gather everyone together and re-establish order. A simple hand up and a well-projected *Game Master says...*brings everyone into focus again. Now this is worth mountains of gold!

Detectives, are there any words you think would be confusing to someone who is reading this poem, any words you think a reader may not know? This deliberate language avoids giving those eager faces a chance to retreat because they fear they are not "smart enough" if they do not know a specific definition. By asking in a way that they are able to think on behalf of others, students also become helpers. If they decide to admit they do not know a word's meaning, that is their choice, not an imperative delivered by the Game Master. This becomes an equalizer and a more positive approach to invite them into the pleasure of discovery that words offer readers.

From this point, we begin to identify words that may be unfamiliar. This is an opportunity to explain that a poem does not just magically appear on the page. Poets are deliberate in making word choices. I stress that there will never be a word in a published poem that is not there on purpose. Each word has a job to do in providing us, the reader detectives, a connection to the poet's intention. Just as some of us know people who work more than one job, so a word can be employed for more than one role. Just as the person with two jobs may have two sets of responsibilities, even different uniforms or other ways to dress, a word may have different jobs, other definitions when it shows up for work in a line, be it a noun, verb, preposition, conjunction, article, adjective, or adverb. This exemplifies a cross-over opportunity to develop general reading comprehension skills beyond the construct of poetry.

To answer the question *What do you think the poet wants us to feel, think, believe, or understand from these words?*, the definition of each word on the page must be clear. Here I return to what I learned from Cris Tovani, a reading comprehension specialist and author of *I Read It, but I Don't Get It*: we are able to help students cultivate ways to recognize the point at which they disconnect from their reading and encourage students to slow down, to be as deliberate in their reading as the writer is in composing the work. I encourage students to rely upon the dictionary, not to slide past a word they don't know in a rush to be done.

Another strategy is to identify "dictionary guides," one or two assistants who are willing to look up words on behalf of the class. It is a responsibility for the collective, a post as important as the scribe in collaborative writing. The dictionary is an enormous ring of keys to new awareness and knowledge. I share that I look up words almost every day.

After we confirm that we are comfortable with the definitions, I select a few students who have not yet had a chance to read and ask them to read the poem aloud again. Sometimes I invite two or three to read in a chorus so the poem becomes thicker to the ear. Sometimes I invite the teacher to read the poem in the way she hears it. I generally read it aloud in the way I hear and comprehend the poem several times throughout our lessons. It is not uncommon for the class to experience a single poem up to 20 times, both silently and aloud, each time discovering something new, before we complete our investigation.

We can search for nouns, pronouns, verbs, modifiers, and discuss the differences. We can pick out certain words and conduct a synonym search. We can discuss conjunctions and past tense versus present tense. We can add written punctuation if there is a poem that relies on visual punctuation, as so many contemporary poems do.

In a week-long residency, I generally wait until the second day of experiencing the poem before we begin to discuss our sense of its meaning and what the poem reminds us of in our own lives. Then the students start to tell their own stories, in which wild, new poems are waiting to be harnessed.

We are almost always mid-stream in a thought when my 45 or 60 minutes are up and I have to move on to another classroom to restart the game with another group of detectives. I quickly review our progress and what we discovered in our session. This then sets up a healthy anticipation for the next day without giving away too much. I rely on the element of surprise, being the jester that I am. In the lower grades, I make a grand gesture of saving the game where we left it and powering down.

After we have discussed the poem to our full satisfaction, we illustrate it. It is generally possible to determine which parts of the poem each child is particularly connected to by observing the artists at work. Similar images in the majority of the pictures will demonstrate shared comprehension of the overall theme. One or two students are likely to construct images no one else draws, providing the chance to talk about the validity of varied responses to a poem. When the artwork is complete, we hang the pictures and stage a "gallery walk" to view all of the drawings while searching for clues that are both similar and different. This "compare and contrast" lesson encourages further discussion about the theme of the poem and seeing firsthand how we all imagine differently, as well as similarly, based on the words presented by the poet.

Often I provide the poem on a small piece of paper for each student to hold and read up close throughout our process. For another bonus level, I assign the following homework: *Put the poem in your bookbag. Take it home and read the poem to an adult. That adult can be a parent, a neighbor, another teacher in an after-school program, a grandparent, or auntie. Read the poem; attempt to generate dialogue based on what you now know and comprehend from the poet. Have your listener sign the poem, bring it back to class tomorrow, and you earn a bonus.* (Some teachers will accept the completed assignment for extra credit as well.)

With middle- and high-school students, though I forgo the thinking cap and badge motif, I rely upon the same metaphor of the video-game process. This approach works with young people, who seem to accept failure in a video game in ways they do not in other contexts. It is no big deal to be "killed" in a game and have to start again, each time becoming wiser about the pitfalls at each level. Since I stress that there is no "wrong" in the game, students know there are no penalties for incorrect responses. This is a game in which a player always moves forward and may return to a previous level simply to review a clue. It may be a way to plant seeds for future reading habits.

As I move from class to class, the game changes with the temperament of the class as a whole, how the teacher manages the class, the time of day, etc. One additional tool I have as Game Master is the competition between classes. I can simply drop a hint that another class made it to Level 16 by day two and I have a forest of hands before me from which I can select a new reader. Both students and teachers always want to top the other classes.

If the residency is long enough, we will also write poems using a similarly tiered approach, breaking down the writing process into levels as well. I write my expectations and instructions on the board one at a time, repeating the direction several times and asking students to repeat my instructions in their own words. If an interactive Whiteboard is available, I develop a lesson-plan template with each level of instruction presented as a separate, sequential slide. If I am teaching in a school that supplies daily planners, I ask students to record the objectives there as well so they remember the requirements for homework later.

In my elementary school video-game residencies, I love to work with Kay Ryan's "Bear Song," due to its fabulous metaphors and intriguing word choices. (A more detailed investigation of this poem is presented in the essay "Grasping for Imagination in the Face of Fear" on p. 117). Among the poems accessible to elementary-, middle-, and high-school students alike, I am quite fond of Langston Hughes' "I, too, sing America." In the course of examining Hughes' 62 modest and well-chosen words under the microscope, we unearth the consequences of deep segregation and northern migration of Black Americans throughout the 20th Century. We discuss the generations of people of African descent who have worked as domestics and laborers in the homes of White middle- and upper-class American, raising children and maintaining grounds and vehicles other than their own, echoing the scars of slavery as an institution and economic foundation of a relatively new nation. There is so much history in Hughes' words to share with our youth.

Nikki Giovanni's "Knoxville, Tennessee" has become another of my favorites to teach. This poem is as universal to Americans as the song published in 1940, "You Are My Sunshine." No matter the age or region of the country, no matter the economic class or size of the community, this poem builds its bridge to almost every reader.

Knoxville, Tennessee

I always like summer
best
you can eat fresh corn
from daddy's garden
and okra
and greens
and cabbage

and lots of barbecue
and buttermilk
and homemade ice-cream
at the church picnic
and listen to
gospel music
outside
at the church
homecoming
and go to the mountains with
your grandmother
and go barefooted
and be warm
all the time
not only when you go to bed
and sleep

What a miracle this poem is for a teacher. What a lovely scenario with all of its nuance for the reader. Seventy-one words, including title, "Knoxville, Tennessee" is masterful in the way it provides opportunities for investigation:

Level One: Ask student to read the poem silently two times.

Level Two: Have it read aloud with different voices at least three times.

Level Three: The teacher or resident poet recites the poem for the class with inflection to invite another interpretation.

Level Four: First inquiry: *What words do you find in the poem that you believe would be confusing to a reader, or that a reader might not understand? Are there any words that make you question why the poet chose them?*

Ah yes, now we start the questioning! We highlight the level-four words on the screen or write them on the board. The list commonly includes *buttermilk, barbecue, gospel music, homecoming*, and my favorite, *okra*. I have learned to bring in a quart of buttermilk and small cups for sampling and fresh okra to examine. We discuss church choirs singing in magnificent harmony, church hats; we compare family gatherings and reunions.

Then I get to share the story of okra, a tale that was further developed in winter 2010 with the research of a group of sixth-graders and their teacher, my partners in discovery for 10 days. Okra is common to gumbo and jambalaya. Okra swims in Indian curries and lies pickled in jars on Food Lion shelves. We order it fried in chicken shacks and soul-food restaurants. Some of us have eaten it since we were kids. Some people have never even seen it. I always thought okra looked like the 7-ounce Coke bottles of my childhood, the ones with the cities in which the soda was bottled stamped into the glass bottom. Bottles we collected to see how many states we could gather, or to get back nickel deposits at the corner store that we could trade for bubblegum packs with baseball cards or full-sized Milky Ways. In the summers of my childhood, one bottle equaled a refreshing Fudgesicle on a lazy afternoon.

But what about the origin of okra? Where did that small vegetable pod with a shell fuzzy like a kiwi, seeds like tapioca, and a slimy goo that wards off many diners actually come from? The answer is Africa.

Imagine ourselves in the garden in West Africa one morning hundreds of years ago. Suddenly we are ripped from our village, away from our home, maybe our family or maybe our whole community is kidnapped. One of us has a pod or two of okra clutched in hand. We then gaze around the inside of the slave castles, and through the doors of no return at the endless ocean.

The horror of the Middle Passage is graphic and engrossing as we consider being chained together prone in the belly of a ship likely not larger than the area of approximately three or four average classrooms. The sounds become deafening, sickening. One of us has found a way to keep that okra pod close, perhaps hidden in the folds of a skirt or still tightly wrapped in a fist.

Those of us who survived the journey across the Atlantic are sold on the auction block as property, a father to one bidder, mother to another, brothers and sisters split, never to see each other again. Everything is unfamiliar, frightening, and nothing is easy. There are few choices and we, a once proud people, are treated with no more regard than a horse or milk cow. Still, one of us suffered through the indignities with that okra pod safely transported.

On some plantation or smaller farm somewhere in the southern part of this young nation still defining itself, our courageous brother or sister finds a place in the soil for a small pile of dried white seeds to yield a small plot of one vegetable from home. More are dried and shared with other families. Season after season we plant again, the flavor and memory of Africa kept alive. More and more seeds are shared with other humans suffering the shameful fate of chattel slavery. Then the taste is shared with the "big house" of the plantation owner's family.

And now, generations and dramatic histories later, we commonly find okra in American supermarkets from Alabama to Alaska. We can buy it in small cardboard boxes in the frozen food aisle, we can find fresh okra and hand select the most tender pods for dinner. We enjoy okra without considering one person's quiet, heroic act of perseverance just to keep a bond with home, a home he or she would never see again. A home that would dissolve into dream.

The levels of discovery from this point are up to you. I will pull every drop of personal connection I possibly can, awarding additional levels of achievement to the class for each side trip we take in our conversations that yields understanding, each time we return to the pure language of the words to listen to the poem aloud, our subsequent discussions about how we envision the scene or scenes from our own lives that mirror the poem.

Then the question that will lead me to the happy dance. We count the number of words at this point. *What word of those 69 (title not included) stands out the most?* The answer is quite simple: *AND. How many times do we find the word AND?* After various counts, we come to agree on the sum 11. *Now what would make a poet, someone who is deliberate about language, someone who would expect every word in a poem to earn its way into the whole, what would cause that poet to repeat that word 11 times in a poem that is only 69 words long?*

How many of you have little brothers and sisters? Annoying brothers and sisters who walk in your room without knocking. Aggravating siblings who just can't wait to tell you about whatever happened today at school, on the playground, in the backyard just now?

Hands shoot into the air. I ask for volunteers to imitate those little kids. The single run-on sentence goes on and on...perhaps for 60-plus words with gasps here and there for emphasis.

And what is the most common word in each of these stories?

The class is a single chorus of "OOOOOOOHHHHHH! AND!"

They've got it! Bonus level! Happy dancing poet!

Once in a while a student realizes this clue without prompt or well ahead of the rest of the class. That bright star will be the hero of the day because he or she will earn the award of a level or two (depending on my mood) on behalf of the whole class.

Now we all hear little Nikki, the child that she was, the captured memory that caused young poet Nikki to put pen to paper, the voice that once was, and now remains immortal. With this example, we can write our own memories building on Ms. Giovanni's model as a sturdy foundation.

Once we have immersed in all of the sensory components, the family traditions, the meals and childhood memories, once we have compared our experience with that of the poet, I instruct the students to share the poem that evening at home.

The next day some students have forgotten, some leave the poems signed on the kitchen table, some parents complain, some are indifferent. Once a student came back to class to say that when they discussed the poem, his dad got so hungry he made a big fried-chicken dinner for the family. What better praise could I ask for and what better reward for sharing a poem?

In utilizing this method as a model for inquiry, after assessing that students have a firm grasp of the context thus far, the teacher or teaching artist may adapt the process to suit students' needs and grade level, and to meet the scope and sequence of curriculum and learning standards. I pull every drop of personal connection possible, awarding additional levels of achievement to the class for each side trip we take in our conversations that yields understanding, each time we return to the pure language of the words to listen to it aloud, and throughout our subsequent discussions about how we envision the scene or scenes from our own lives that mirror the poem.

The highest compliment, a clear mark of success, will come from students themselves. One morning, I had run overtime with a third-grade class. I scrambled to find the things I had scattered around the room: my clipboard with my schedule, a highlighter, my water bottle, my bookbag. As I opened the door, bidding goodbye until tomorrow, one boy yelled out, "Wait, Ms. Popoff, you can't leave yet! You forgot to save the game!"

COMPREHENSIVE LESSON PLAN

Recipe for a Simple Start: Poem of the Week

Georgia A. Popoff

Objective: To develop a daily practice of using poetry in the classroom that will build student competence in reading comprehension and in drawing inferences from written material.

Applicable Age/Grade Level: This method is applicable to all age groups and grade levels.

Anticipated Time: One poem per week, five to 10 minutes daily throughout the school year.

Materials/Resources Needed: A selection of poems to be reproduced as small, individual handouts for students, a sheet of chart paper, Post-it notes.

Process Overview:
The Poem of the Week practice will work best if initiated at the beginning of the school year and continued weekly. Once the class is accustomed to the process, the discussions can become as short as just five minutes a day, though it may take a bit longer at the beginning.

Preparation:

- Select a poem for the week, approximately 10-15 lines. You can visit websites such as Teachers & Writers Collaborative, Ted Kooser's American Life in Poetry, Billy Collins' Poetry 180, Poetry Out Loud, the Academy of American Poets, and The Poetry Foundation, among other resources, for poems that are thematically and linguistically appropriate for the age/grade level you are teaching. Include poetry written by young people as well, so that students can have models written by their peers. One source for wonderful poetry by young writers is Richard Lewis' anthology, *Miracles*. You can also access the annual Scholastic student writing anthologies for examples.

- Create a handout of the poem, rather than having students read it in a book. This permits a closer connection and takes the poem out of its expected environment, isolating it for deeper inspection.

- Create a projection or interactive Whiteboard file with the poem, if the technology is available.

Day One:

- Ask the class to read the poem on the handout twice silently. Read the poem aloud to the class once as they read along, then invite students to read it aloud with you.
- On a piece of chart paper hung in a consistent, easy-to-reach location, create a "Vocabulary Parking Lot." Have students place Post-it notes with words used in the poem that they do not know written on them. This becomes the week's vocabulary list, or adds to the weekly essential vocabulary. Discuss the words or assign students to find definitions in a way that suits the classroom need and timing for daily instruction. Encourage students to review the parking lot throughout the week to see if they have struggled with the same words as others or if they can define any of the words for the class.

Day Two:

- Read the poem aloud to the class again, while the students read along from the handout or from the board. Ask one or two students also to read the poem aloud.
- Ask students to identify parts of speech and other phonemic aspects in the poem. For instance, start the discussion by asking

students to find the nouns that they recognize in the poem. Continue to locate verbs, pronouns, articles, etc. This is an opportunity to engage in a brief discussion of the meaning of the vocabulary parking lot words.

Day Three:

- Have a student read the poem aloud to the class again, while the others read it on the handout.

- Ask students to identify and discuss aspects of the poem that illustrate literary elements, such as figurative language and form. You can start by asking students to point out descriptive language in the poem, or how sound is used through techniques such as alliteration, assonance, consonance, rhyme, etc., or what sensory details are employed within the poem to "paint the picture" for the reader.

Day Four:

- Have another student read the poem aloud to the class, while the class reads it on the handout.

- Start a short discussion regarding the theme of the poem, what students think the poet is asking them to believe, and how they feel about the poet's viewpoint. Allow differing points of view to be expressed and explained, helping students to recognize the subjective potential of a poem as a work of art.

Day Five:

- Have another student read the poem aloud to the class, while the class reads it on the handout, purely for enjoyment.

- Engage the class in a short discussion of their responses and interpretations of the poem now that they have experienced it from many different angles, as well as reading and hearing it multiple times throughout the week. Ask students how their impressions of the poem have changed since the first reading on Day One.

Note: Although, for this process, selecting shorter poems is recommended to help keep the daily discussion brief, students will be able to apply what they learn in the shorter pieces to develop more sophisticated responses when they examine longer poems.

Expected Outcomes:

- Develops stronger vocabulary.

- Increases reading comprehension.

- Strengthens critical-thinking skills through inquiry-based examination of poems.

- Increases competency in addressing abstract thought and metaphor in order to draw inference from the content.

- Creates greater familiarity with a variety of poets and styles of writing.

- Teaches students to support each other in learning, sharing ideas and concepts, and strengthening writing skills.

COMPREHENSIVE LESSON PLAN

Six-Word Memoir Self-Portrait

Georgia A. Popoff

Objective: To offer students an opportunity for self-reflection and expression of emotions, sensibilities, and beliefs through writing a five- or six-stanza poem that reflects effective writing practices, economy of language, deliberate word choice, understanding of poetic elements, and improved vocabulary.

Applicable Age/Grade Level: This lesson is adaptable to all age groups and grade levels, dependent on competency in writing skills.

Anticipated Time: Adaptable, from two 45-minute sessions to a week-long process.

Materials/Resources Needed: Copy of at least one of the Six-Word Memoir anthologies as reference, writing materials (paper, pen/pencil), dictionary, thesaurus. If the technology is available, refer to the *SMITH Magazine* website (*www.smithmag.net*) to project examples. [Note: there is now an anthology of teen memoirs and a designated website for student posting that will limit the possibility of age-inappropriate content.]

Process Overview:

The Six-Word Memoir Self-Portrait activity can be completed in two to five sessions with the first day focused on introduction to the form and students writing their first responses to the prompts. On the second day, students flesh out the six-word memoirs into longer poems. Poems may be revised and finalized on the third day, or as a homework assignment. If time permits, a fourth day can focus on peer critique in pairs or small groups, with a fifth day for students to read their work to the entire class.

Initiating the Writing Process:

Share a few six-word memoirs from one of the anthologies or the websites as models and start a discussion by commenting on how a few words can depict many ideas, concepts, and emotions.

- Instruct the students to take out a piece of paper and a pen or pencil.

- Offer the first prompt: *Who are you right this minute? Remember to say it in just six words.* The response can be a list of adjectives or a phrase or two; it does not need to be a complete sentence. Advise students to limit their use of articles, conjunctions, and personal pronouns.

- Ask the students to skip four or five lines on the paper and reply to a second prompt (e.g., *Who were you at 7:00 AM today?*). Then ask them to skip four or five lines on the page again. These blank lines will provide the space where students will build out their stanzas.

- Repeat this process until you have first lines, all six-word memoirs, for five or six stanzas that will later include four lines each—quatrains—as in the models below. Be creative in thinking of writing prompts. As a starting point, questions like the following can help students identify milestones and significant ages and events that shaped their personalities:

- Who were you last Friday?

- Who will you be at 3:00 PM today?

- Who will you be tonight when your head is on your pillow at the last moment before you sleep?

- Who were you on the first day of school in September? Kindergarten? Middle school?

- Who will you be after you graduate from high [or elementary/ middle] school?

- Who were you when you took a big risk?

- Who are you when you are participating in something you really love (e.g., sports, dancing, cooking, listening to music, swimming)?

- Who were you when you did something you are really proud of or something that you now regret?

Drafting the Poem:

Once the students' lists are complete, give instructions for the structure of the stanzas.

- Each stanza will have four lines. The first line will be six words and the other three of any length. These additional lines should further tell the story of the six-word memoir on the first line.

- Include at least one simile or metaphor in lines two to four of each stanza.

- Each stanza should describe one sound that is related to the narrative and not human (e.g., a car engine, a wolf howling, a door slamming).

- Each stanza should include one smell or aroma associated with the memory.

- Be sure to include at least one adjective and/or adverb in each stanza.

- After all of the stanzas are complete, add one final six-word memoir that sums up the autobiographical picture

- The result is a five-stanza, 21-line poem or a six-stanza, 26-line poem.

Revising for Success:
Ask students to:

- Review their poems while identifying words for which synonyms may be substituted that better illustrate the theme of each stanza.

- Edit the poems for all elements of writing: punctuation, spelling, grammar, etc.

[**Note:** Peer critique may be included in the revision process to allow students to reflect and respond to the effectiveness of each other's work prior to finalizing their drafts.]

Finalizing the Draft:
Ask students to type their poems in the computer lab or at home, nada to proofread their work before handing it in.

Publication and Performance:
This element is up to the individual teacher and class, as time, budget, and circumstance permit. Creating a class anthology, an in-class reading, a "poetry café" school performance, or family-oriented performance event are all options.

Expected Outcomes:

- Development of writing skills, vocabulary, and knowledge of required elements of English language arts and poetry as a genre.

- Self-reflection and self-awareness expressed creatively.

- Empathy for others through sharing poems written in class, as well as the models provided.

Model for Poetic Structure [Note: These examples take liberties with the stated form.]:

Example 1:   A girl, stressed out, cause: school
                School seems like a jail
                I am waiting, anxious, stressed, to take the test
                Waiting for fourth period

Example 2:   Bored confused—until track practice starts.
                We run around town and see homeless in carts.
                It's really hard and they put you to the test.
                But you gotta work if you want to be the best.

POETRY AND CURRICULUM CONNECTIONS

Inquiry and Reflection in the Core Subjects

INTRODUCTION

Georgia A. Popoff & Quraysh Ali Lansana

Poetry and its creation lend themselves readily, in fact exceptionally well, as adjuncts to other core content areas in K–12 curricula. Poetry can be used as a learning and assessment tool in core subjects beyond English language arts. Innovative methods to teach and learn may be achieved, in such ways as:

- Studying an era of history or geographic area through the voices of the poets of that time or place;

- Creating poems that tell stories learned during a social studies unit;

- Investigating poetic rhyme and meter and the correlation to mathematical patterns; examining and expressing the similar observation methods of scientists and poets.

Reading poems with themes that mirror the subject matter in standard textbooks provides students with a different way to comprehend and retain information. Social studies, including history, geography, sociology, economics, and political science, becomes more palpable when poetry is used to illustrate the era, location, circumstance, or key figures students are studying. Reading the work of Basho, coupled with biographical detail, will further students' experience of 17th-Century Japan. A study of Central and South America might incorporate the works of Jorge Luis Borges, Pablo Neruda, Nicanor Parra, and Octavio Paz. The struggle of North America's indigenous peoples is reflected in the poetry of many native writers, including Joy Harjo, Sherman Alexie, and Mark Turcotte. A simple poem by Langston Hughes or Gwendolyn Brooks can depict many elements of American history, as can the work of Walt Whitman.

Great potential and value exist in students writing creatively within another discipline or subject area. For instance, if we imagine an arbitrary situation, say a baseball game, and place noted characters from history and science in the bleachers at that game, then ask students to create a poem in the voice of that historical figure in that moment, what may be witnessed? Will students reflect the quality of their learning? Will they be able to do research and learn more to meet teachers' expectations?

It can be equally effective to have students write in the voice of a figure from the past, but within the relevant context. Asking a student to write a poem in the voice of Marie Curie as she was on the brink of a major breakthrough in her experimentation not only affords the chance to articulate her process as a scientist, but also to demonstrate an understanding of how chemical compounds work together. This demands of the student a more organic tie to the elements of the physical world than requiring rote memorization of the Periodic Table

What if teachers take the more abstract elements of science or math—pi or an imaginary number, the golden ratio, the speed of light—and then challenge students to develop metaphoric reflections of these concepts in verse? Students can create poems that embody subject matter, rather than merely describing it.

Many educators look for new angles on standard or stale lesson plans. Poems with themes illustrating the concepts of any core content area offer conduits to retention of the lesson. The good news is that for centuries poets have crafted verse about most everything under the sun. Students and teachers have a vast reservoir of poems at their disposal to study for inspiration and as source material. A simple library visit or Internet search will provide countless responses to queries for poems about geometry, algebra, chemistry, history, political science, and more. In our work as teaching artists and professional development consultants, we have utilized selections from poets as varied as Carl Sandburg, A. Van Jordan, Li-Young Lee, Martha Collins, Ann Silsbee, Federico García Lorca, and Brian Turner. One of our favorites is Rita Dove's poem "Geometry."

Geometry

I prove a theorem and the house expands:
the windows jerk free to hover near the ceiling,
the ceiling floats away with a sigh.

As the walls clear themselves of everything
but transparency, the scent of carnations
leaves with them. I am out in the open

and above the windows have hinged into butterflies,
sunlight glinting where they've intersected.
They are going to some point true and unproven.

The poem here is "the thing," the language itself represents a geometric progression. Metaphorically, we see lines, angles, and shapes that are both constant and changing. There is a process of inquiry and resulting discovery, as well as implication of the value of both. The poem investigates the joy of proving a theory with all its opportunities for understanding.

Writing a poem about a subject that students have studied requires them to distill source information and ideas. As a result, assigning students to write poems that articulate learned concepts has value as an assessment strategy. When we ask students to translate the learning from any chapter in a textbook or unit of study into poetic thought, there is an additional process of understanding source material through creative expression. It may be likened to the translation of a poem from Spanish to English, or changing a toy car into a Transformer robot. The literal articulation of source material in a prose report or essay may be as flat as a word-for-identical-word translation of Pablo Neruda or the Indian mystic poet Mirabai. There is a lost magic. The need to create a poem encourages moving 20 degrees left or right of the subject matter to allow imagination to take over.

Based on most teachers' familiarity with the literary arts, we believe that poetry is an art form that makes a first leap into arts-integrated activities easier for the classroom teacher, as opposed to other artistic genres and media. Poetry then provides a natural link to other fine arts. Once created, a poem can be danced, transformed into theater, sung, illustrated in visual media and graphic arts, or animated in video. The foundation for all these artistic possibilities is creative expression. When a painter is in the studio, he is thinking in terms of image. A choreographer is articulating time and space. A singer is giving resonance and interpretation to lyrics. All of these elements may be found within the stanzas of writers across many centuries.

Both reading and writing poetry can be used in instruction across the curriculum. In presenting subject matter, include poetry written on the theme being studied; poems can depict data, description, fact, and conjecture in an imaginative way that effectively supplements more "academic" texts. Poetry is both experience and translation of that experience to others. This simple poem by the late Ann Silsbee illustrates this quite gently.

Trails
for J.M.

Ninety-three million miles away
sunspots surface from the sunfire
flaming just a little cooler than the whole.
Their darkness boils with light they are again
becoming. We see their cold magnetic glow
in northern skies on star-hung nights.
Streaks of color thrum through the blues
of atmosphere after the sun itself
has sunk behind hills. When the bands fade
something like music still shimmers on.

You were always flame, your brightness
just a little dimmer than the whole,
like ours.

Detours and the Teachable Moment

Georgia A. Popoff

Hate is a human habit that is learned and inherited.
Keep walking forward.
—Popoff Whiteboard
notes, April 2007

teach the way I drive. I have a route planned when I turn the key in the ignition, but if traffic conditions, my mood, road construction, or weather conditions require detours, I change my course. In fact, it has always been my habit to learn multiple routes to most destinations, especially if the drives are a part of my routine. I prefer to minimize my time at stoplights, so I look for ways to avoid them. I pay attention to traffic patterns and how they play out at different times of day. I prefer to avoid obstacles and seize chances to spice up my life with variety and changes in the landscape.

Sometimes I walk into a classroom with one lesson plan set to go and it becomes obvious that I am faced with a detour. I also enjoy following the students' lead. If an unexpected and miraculous teachable moment presents itself, I am all for dropping one current to follow another.

One fall I walked to the last classroom at the end of the corridor of the seventh-grade house of a sprawling middle school. I had taught with the host teacher the previous year. We are chronological peers, Boomers with our idealism periodically on hold due to the realities of working for a living. This teacher is one of many teaching veterans who is witnessing the creativity of her craft desiccated by the current climate of education. When she puts in her request for my class visits during my residency in the school, we know each other well enough that we can teach what and how we want, curriculum be damned. It is the only time during this teacher's school year that she can escape the rigors of her daily planner.

I cannot explain just how it happened, but something came to mind in my preliminary conversation with this particular class of seventh-graders that detoured us from my expectations for the day. I was aware that several schools in which I taught, including this one, were assigning to English classes a young-adult novel with a plot based on the Japanese internment camps of the 1940s. I asked if any of these students were familiar with this dark secret of American history. Of course, no one knew anything about it so there I was, a visiting poet scheduled for a literacy class, teaching 20th-Century American history. Again.

I am from a family in which discourse and opinion are valued. My father was an intellectually curious man and his politics were ingrained in all of my siblings and myself. We argued about economics and the existence of God over meals. We still do. We are a family deeply opposed to racial discrimination to the point that my father and one of our neighbors—the father of the second Black family to move onto our modest middle-class block—staged their own sit-in at a neighborhood diner in our upstate New York small city that would not serve African Americans. On October 15, 1969, one day before my sixteenth birthday, my dad put his job as a technical writer with top security clearance at General Electric on the line to march with his kids in the local protest held on the same day as the national Moratorium march in Washington, DC. As a man who had fought in "the war to end all wars" in his late teens, he was compelled to lend his presence and voice in opposition to the Vietnam War, three of his children walking beside him, a fourth carried on his shoulders.

I continue to be an activist, one who works with young people. In spite of growing up in a politically conscious environment, I remember how uninformed about the world around me I truly was as a teen. I now seize every chance to share those hard-to-access bits of history that slip past textbook editors and curriculum designers. I often teach the history I lived. This moment with the seventh-graders was one of those opportunities.

I provided an overview of the atrocity of American citizens of Japanese descent being rounded up, severed from homes, businesses, fruitful lives to be shipped to remote parts of the country and warehoused like livestock. I described the sub-standard housing and the barbed wire, the limited food supplies, and the cold winters. I asked if this reminded anyone of other circumstances they had heard of before. Someone answered that Hitler's Germany was the same. I agreed and we discussed how we cannot really imagine what either event would feel like. I told the tale of the first Holocaust survivor I met, and how I was the students' age when I first noticed the numbers tattooed on his arm.

I wanted to poke at the source of our disconnection from the horror. Internment camps, concentration camps, these are the same thing or very similar. *What was the problem with those words?* I asked. We looked at the word *camp*. That was it! *What are camps to us generally? Basketball or football camp, skate camp, sports camp, or camping in the woods, all summer activities to look forward to, right? What about boot camp?* Not quite as much fun but, still, not imprisonment. Not desperate, desolate isolation where death is imminent. None of the camps with which we were familiar carried a mission of dehumanization. We were on a roll! Then I shared stories of the trans-Atlantic slave trade and the Middle Passage.

We cited these three separate times in history in which we were aware of humans totally negating the humanity of others based on skin tone, religion, and cultural heritage. Then I asked for an example from the present day in which people fear other people just because of their religion or culture. The class agreed that Muslims, particularly Arabs, worldwide were experiencing the same types of atrocity and prejudice.

My improvised plan formulated instantaneously. The class was instructed to divide itself into four groups by personal interest in the circumstances we had been discussing. The charge to each group was to collaborate to create a poetic piece, with the intention of performing the work by week's end. Each poem was to be written in the voice of a person or people of the demographic and circumstance the group was studying—a persona poem. For the first evening's homework, the students would be responsible for doing research on their chosen topic to share with the other members of their creative team the next day.

On Tuesday, I would expect the students to share facts and data, to look for threads upon which to build a persona poem speaking in the voices of those who lived what they were studying. They just had to share research and composition. Wednesday would be brainstorming and first drafts. Thursday would be revision. Friday would involve quick rehearsal and presentation. The poems could be presented any way they chose; there could be parts assigned to different readers, a choral ensemble, or one student could represent the whole.

In the course of the discussion, somehow we got on the subject of the march on Jena, Louisiana, planned that week in 2007 to protest the arrest of the "Jena Six," a group of Black high-school students convicted in the beating of a White student. Other than two media hounds in class, my seventh-graders did not know a thing about this current event, and even the two who did were really not sure why this was news and why the young Black men were initially charged with attempted second-degree murder. The teacher and I had no such confusion. We are old enough to have witnessed the images of the Civil Rights Era conflicts and actions on our black-and-white TV screens as we grew up. This incident playing out throughout the week on cable and network news was an immediate illustration of the fact that racism is not relegated to history. It is still evident in our lives. I assigned a side job to the two students who were somewhat familiar with the case. They were to monitor the march and bring what they discovered to class as daily reports.

We first had to parse out why Black students would be offended about a noose or not being able to sit under a tree, the only shade tree on the school campus. Why was it such a big deal? I drew a noose on the board along with some other symbols. We discussed the power of icons and visual symbols in general. We talked about how symbols work in marketing, in politics, and in brainwashing. We talked about the stars that German Jews were forced to wear in public; then the color coding of stars for others offensive to the Third Reich: the pink stars displayed on the chests of Germans known to be gay, for instance. I then spoke of the approximately 3,200 lynchings of Black Americans in the 19th and 20th centuries. The noose became more than a knot. We were all electric with indignation and outrage.

Many of the students were of color. This was the first time I made my point of equality and diversity by pointing out the seemingly White males and then asking them to stand. I established these few young men as examples of those who would be the only ones permitted education in the 1800s, an approach that rarely fails me in capturing attention. Afterward, one of the young men told me that he "passed" because I took him to be of European descent. In fact, he was Irish on one side of the family but the other was Puerto Rican. Another lesson for me to remember not to presume. Still, I made my point about how we should never take our freedom or our education for granted.

Thursday I circulated among the clusters of students as they revised their poems and started to work on staging for the next day. The empathy at work in each group was remarkable, as was the spirit of collaboration. This was far better than what I thought we would be doing together at this point of the week. The teacher was beaming as she checked work, asked questions, and offered suggestions to each of the clusters. We were in teaching heaven.

On Friday we first talked about the march and our right as members of a democracy to challenge injustice. We discussed the failures of societies that outlaw opinion and choice. We affirmed that we are all responsible for the unity of our neighborhoods, schools, cities—anything regarding community is our sacred trust as citizens to uphold. Then the students performed their work. It was extraordinary. It was a magnificent moment of a September afternoon, the leaves reflecting the diversity of the poets before me, and of the nation in which we live. The students' poems and their commitment to the work made me cry. The language choice was conscious and effective in each poem. The students were fully immersed in the performances. The statements of understanding were profound. Something remarkable had happened. I will always remember that I was moved to tears.

As we ended class that Friday, I asked the poets to consider what it takes to save a community from situations like that of the march on Jena, Louisiana, that fall. I captured the comments with a dry-erase marker as we spoke. I saved the pictures of the scrawls on the board from throughout the week. *How do WE change things?* The comments that continue to resonate with me include:

- Stop judging others.
- We are all equally human.
- Stop the violence.
- Discuss the problem.

109

- Research history.
- Stay educated.
- Share your knowledge.

'Nuff said.

PERSONA AND THE CLASSROOM

Writing in the Voices of Others

Georgia A. Popoff & Quraysh Ali Lansana

VI.

if you don't know who you are, anybody can
name you.

—Haki R. Madhubuti,
Liberation Narratives

Acting is a natural state of being human. As children, we identify with familial roles, superheroes, athletes, military and law enforcement officers; and we play make believe, setting up elaborate scenarios to act out, directing each other in dialogue and response, even creating stages or sets for our imagined lives. It is a commonly held concept in performance-studies programs that performance occurs every day in ordinary life. As we ride the bus or the subway and watch a mother soothe her crying baby or scream at the child, each of the woman's choices and actions is performance, as is our observation of the mother and child. When we advise the young people in our lives to behave appropriately at a sleepover or during an outing with friends at the mall, we are asking them to assume a role that fits time and place, rather than moving through the world unconsciously.

As we navigate through life, we each wear a series of masks, and we assume varied elements of our personal identities to accommodate the expectations of others. In the classroom, to develop a sense of self-awareness and voice, the following questions may be asked:

- Who were you when you woke up this morning that may be different from who you are now as you occupy that desk?

- Who are you on the basketball court in the park after school?

- Who are you when you visit your grandparents versus who you are when you sit at the lunch table in the cafeteria?

- Who are you when you are in a house of worship and who do you hope to be after graduation?

All of these questions provide an opportunity to take an inventory of the many faces students wear, visages that change throughout the day. For some, this may be the first time they ever think of their own habit of adaptation to setting and circumstance.

A poem may be like putting on a winter coat or a suit of armor. Persona poetry, the poem written in the voice and from the outlook of another, lends itself to this donning of clothing or costume because it is already based in a point of view beyond the poet's own. The Greek root of the word persona means *mask*. This poetic form presents the voice of another, either animate or inanimate, as that entity responds to a specific place, time, and situation, either real or imagined. A persona poem offers a way to articulate knowledge of history, community, or environment. Such poems allow poets to question reactions other than their own in the face of tragedy or elation. Inherent in the process of creating poetry in the voice of another is the idea of empathy, the ability to see through another set of eyes, feel through a distant heart. This becomes another form of acting, of role playing that broadens one's perspective. The stage is a blank piece of paper.

Creating persona poetry is a highly effective tool for writing and assessment in a cross-curricular context. For example, if the assignment is to write a poem in the voice of Louis Pasteur upon his first successful attempt at pasteurization, or to speak as Buzz Aldrin stepping back into the lunar module from the moon's surface, imagination is activated in ways that lecture and rote learning cannot spark. In order to write a poem, if a fourth-grade student must think about what she learned in science about how the Orca whale starts its day, the resulting work demonstrates that learning. After a visit to the Charles H. Wright Museum of African American History in Detroit, if a student must write in the voice of a 17th-Century West-African child torn from his village, we will have a mirror into what that young person has internalized from the exhibit depicting the Middle Passage.

All of these possibilities create options for viewing the world with a wider peripheral vision. Poetry is an art of reflection and response. Poetry often speaks on behalf of others. Persona poetry creates a stage for experimentation and compassion. In addition to sparking creative imagining, it provides opportunities to acquire new knowledge through research regarding the chosen subject and to share that knowledge with others. Persona poems are especially useful in assessing learning because they require students to utilize specifics gathered through research and demonstrating the understanding gleaned. Such poems do not simply describe a person or situation. They depict that person's responses to a set of circumstances. Doing this effectively entails the poet stepping outside herself to connect with the unfamiliar.

Intimate details create the foundation for the successful persona poem, which in turn becomes a vehicle to transport the reader into a world in which a character exists and from which that character speaks. Additionally, to feel authentic, the language choices in a persona poem must be appropriate to the period and nature of the moment in which the character resides.

Persona poetry may help students understand cultures, previous generations, and other world views. A child may value a parent's choices and behaviors more if she is asked to view Mom or Dad as someone outside the roles each may play in daily interaction. A high-school student rooted in one nationality may recognize his similarities to a citizen of a nation on the other side of the globe, thus becoming more accepting of differences as well as cognizant of common threads that exist among humans. This empathy may move young people to acts of philanthropy and activism, concrete action for change. Note this poem by an eleventh-grader, along with how he defines persona and explains why he crafted this particular voice.

> I see the world through two different eyes.
> Symbol of violence between two different sides.
> What was I even constructed for?
> When will they ever end this war?
> One side is brutal, torn down and mean
> The other is fearful, aggressive and weak

A symbol of hate, separation and war
I don't see what I was constructed for.

—Persona poems are written
through the eyes of another person,
animal, or object. They portray
how an object feels about things
and what it would be thinking if it
were alive. I chose this poem
because it is about an important
part of history...the Berlin Wall
because it was the only thing that
saw the situation from both sides.

Persona poetry also lends itself to performance. In reading and interpreting a persona poem, students adopt voices that permit them to travel through time and geography. A young person can stand before the class as a noted historical figure, a favorite animal, or an admired celebrity, projecting elements of self while pretending to be someone or something else. Additionally, by acting out a persona poem written by himself or another, the student is pulled out of his seat, activating both his brain and his body, and anchoring the knowledge. Through acting his poem, this student may also develop a new realization of self-confidence and competency. All of this experiential activity is inspired by language and syntax; thus, persona poetry presents an interactive mode of learning and seeing.

Voicing the Margins

▩

Quraysh Ali Lansana

Western history, for the past several centuries, has generally been written by the oppressor. The published stories of the oppressed are a fairly recent phenomenon in the world's narrative. Many of us who are products of public schools were introduced to the African past via the trans-Atlantic slave trade. In many US textbooks, Africa holds no sustained presence prior to that period. Neither Mansa Musa nor Timbuktu was introduced to my active appetite for knowledge as a junior high school student in Oklahoma. For that matter, the Tulsa Race Riot of 1921, considered to be the destruction of Black Wall Street, was not included in the Oklahoma history class curriculum, although Tulsa is two hours from the town of my birth.

This conundrum can be applied to the histories of Chinese Americans, Japanese Americans, Hispanic Americans, people who identify as Lesbian/Gay//Bisexual/Transgender, and others. Africa, in this context, is both representative and real.

I have, for the past two decades, regularly asked students of varying ages, ethnic backgrounds and subject areas, the following questions: *What was your introduction to Africa? What was the initial image or idea of Africa that you remember?* Quite often, older students reference the original, live-action *Tarzan* television series, while the younger crowd mentions Ethiopian hunger relief infomercials featuring bald children with bloated bellies and bad teeth, while a plump blonde American woman delivers an impassioned plea for money.

Again, in the questions above, Africa is metaphor. Remove Africa and fill in the blank with any culture or community you choose. The responses inform how we think and feel about said culture for years to come, unless we are presented with alternative modes of understanding, especially direct interaction. Poetry offers a gateway for accessing the human perspective of other cultures and geographies. Persona poetry takes that access one step further through the empathetic act of wearing another's skin.

Persona poetry has experienced a renaissance in the past decade, particularly among women poets and poets of color in the 30-to-50 age range. This has been amazing for the literary landscape, but of little surprise to me. We have been giving voice to the margins, filling the gaps in our education.

Literature and creative writing are perched on a precarious ledge in the K-12 curriculum. The writing arts are not included in the core arts disciplines (dance, drama, music, visual art), and as components of English language arts curricula they suffer from an assessment-driven, drive-by, cursory exploration. The comprehensive and inclusive power of art as a method of cross-curricular application is well-documented and under-appreciated. Persona poetry is an effective, engaging method of localizing history.

I spent eight years in two Chicago public schools teaching history, social studies, and current events, and utilizing literature and creative writing as vehicles for instruction. Working with teachers to ascertain their lesson plans, I employed poetry reading and writing, and persona poetry in particular, as ways to enhance and entrench the topic of the week. Robert Hayden's "Runagate Runagate," about fugitive Africans guided to freedom by Harriet Tubman, not only provided contextual links to the historical elements on which students would be tested, it also allowed space and emotion for students to connect personally with the conditions and fears of Africans in search of the "promised land." Though it is not a persona poem, the reading and study of "Runagate Runagate" led to the crafting of verse in the voice of runaways as imagined by students in class.

My incorporation of Hayden's poem led to an understanding of just how profound poetry is in localizing historical events and figures. Tubman, for example, is often discussed either during the slavery/Civil War unit or studied as a part of Black History Month, where a cut-out of her face is neatly displayed above the chalkboard. How much do students actually learn about Harriet, the woman, and the utterly grace-guided, astoundingly brave acts she perpetrated at a time when being woman and Black were both major deficits? Does the length of a marking period allow time for students to ask the truth about Tubman never losing a passenger on her journeys to freedom? Is this realistic, and how might she have felt if she had to fire the revolver in her satchel to send a weary runaway to "heaven"? Persona poetry affords students the time to slow down and parse a moment, then enter that moment to sit a spell. Then we write our way out in the mind and voice of that figure in that moment. Any figure, any time period. What an indelible method of teaching and learning.

The persona form itself offers a bridge between some students' lack of connection to history and a transformative educational moment. Unfortunately, I am not the only educator who has been in a classroom with young people uninterested in the past. A Black teenager in Alabama told me a few years ago he was "never a slave, didn't know no slaves, and was not African in any way." True, he himself was too young to have endured chattel slavery, but the likelihood he knew or even shared bloodlines with descendants of African slaves in Alabama is great. Is the desire for homogenization so significant that the denial of truth is natural as hunger? How can anyone suggest we live in a "post-racial" society while some people challenge whether the Jewish Holocaust really occurred or believe reparations for formerly interned Japanese Americans healed their wounds?

My own fascination with history in general, and Harriet Tubman specifically, was born in attempts to connect dots on a genealogical road map. Sadly, I didn't learn of the Tulsa Race Riot until I moved to Chicago in 1989. Just like the Alabama teenager, I was a victim of what information is privileged by whom, and I chose to remain in the relative comfort of that faulty knowledge for far too long. Some people take up residence in ignorance until they perish.

Persona poetry is one among many modes of broadening the learning experience by making history personal. In truth, it already is. Humans are just easily distracted.

In his essay "The Literature of Black America—The Noise of Reading," Dr. William W. Cook writes:

> If language is more than mere word, gesture, tonal
> variation, and so on, literature is more than the sum
> of the words and events which it includes.
> Literature, employing language as one of its
> components, offers readers an image of the world, a

culture. It reflects not only the world of the readers,
but connects that world to other possible worlds.
At its best, it gives the readers a clearer
understanding of themselves and the culture in
which they live.

Persona poetry not only provides images and connections to other worlds, it also gives student writers the authority to create those worlds breath by breath through depicting a particular individual, whether pop star or historical figure. This becomes a profound method of understanding themselves and their own culture, as Cook suggests. For example, one of Harriet Tubman's infamous quotes reads *I would have freed thousands more, if they knew they were slaves.* Certainly, given the time period and her line of work, most students could easily identify the literal context for this statement. Some Black-American captives lacked the desire or necessity to flee. How might young people find relevance for Tubman's words in the early part of the 21st Century? What might Tubman encounter while attempting to recruit runaways in downtown Detroit or on the West Side of Chicago? Where might she find today's "promised land"? What words, tones, or gestures would she employ to convey a sense of urgency?

The aforementioned authority exists in the creative imagining of Tubman's internal and/or external dialogue while she goes door to door on Woodward Avenue in Detroit. She can say whatever the writer wants her to say within the world of the poem. The authority exists in the construction of the specific environment in which she performs these freedom acts. The authority exists in the connection of worlds, past, present, and future.

Longtime friend and poet Tyehimba Jess, author of *leadbelly*, a critically-acclaimed, award-winning book of persona poems on the life of the groundbreaking blues musician, shared that his investment in the form is based upon telling the stories of those forgotten, neglected, or whose lives were lost in translation by dominant culture. "You done taken my blues and gone," as Langston Hughes put it.[1] Persona poetry requires ownership of subject matter through investigation and habitation, not revisionist history.

---

[1] Hughes, Langston. "Note on Commercial Theatre," 1949.

GRASPING FOR IMAGINATION IN THE FACE OF FEAR

Georgia A. Popoff

> Once feeling is neglected, learning cannot become
> process, thought cannot become knowledge. Our
> humanness exists in the recognition of feeling—
> and to live otherwise is to debase and deny our
> struggle to be human.
> —Richard Lewis, *When Thought is Young:*
> *Reflections on Teaching and the Poetry of the Child*

All four heads were bent to the paper in a flurry of inspiration as I approached the cluster of desks. Or so I thought. While three of the fourth-grade students in the cluster were writing with great dedication, another was still, head bowed, pencil stunned. The boy turned up to me, his handsome face still a bit round with childhood in spite of the fact that the day before, when he stood, he looked me straight in the eyes. Today he was brimming with sadness, two streaks marking the lengths of his cheeks.

This was day three of five. The class project, which related to a recent science unit, was to develop persona poems based on animals. On day one, we discussed our project goals as a class. Then the students selected the animals that each would depict based on personal preference and information they had learned from their studies. This English-language-arts project created an opportunity for the teacher to assess what the students had gained from the science unit.

On day one, I also used a terrific poem by Kay Ryan called "Bear Song" from *Poetry Speaks to Children* as a model, not only to examine elements of poetry and the nature of metaphor, but also to explore how writers can bring an animal to life with words.

Bear Song

If I were a bear
with a bear sort of belly

that made it hard
to get up after sitting

and if I had paws
with pads on the ends

and a kind of a tab
where a tail might begin

and a button eye
on each side of my nose

I'd button the flap
of the forest closed.

And when you came
with your wolf and your stick

to the place that once was
the place to get in

you'd simply be
at the edge of the town

and your wolf wouldn't know
a bear was around.

Simple vocabulary discussions of words such as *tab, pad, button,* and *flap* help students see the multiple roles that words play in their many definitions. Then, looking at phrases such as "and a button eye / on each side of my nose" or "I'd button the flap / of the forest closed" provide first steps into breaking down a rather sophisticated metaphor into a digestable concept.

Since the students had completed much of their research prior to my arrival, we spent day two in the library, re-checking facts and preparing to draft work that would become the students' poems. Each day was a step in the direction of a piece that they could share with their peers and that illustrated both the knowledge acquired and their active imaginations, which gave them the ability to place themselves in the role of another—in this case an animal from a habitat vastly different from their environs.

Early in the week, this tearful child had declared that he wanted to be a penguin. It is never a pleasure to witness a child crying, but why was he in tears while all of his classmates were engaged with their poems? In spite of my pain on his behalf, I smiled and asked what could be so upsetting. He whimpered, "I have no imagination."

Here was one of those moments in teaching that causes me to take a deep breath. Imagination is the realm of youth and here was a child obviously distressed because he believed that he lacked something natural to all children. He could see the class of 25 busy at work, calling out, *Miss...come look...is this good?* He watched the other three students in his cluster, shiny black scrawls filling each of their pages like fleet wings across a noon sky. He recognized that he was stuck and believed himself to be the only student who could not do what I asked, such a lonely post. I had to be gentle and affirming, particularly because we'd met only two days earlier.

I responded to his simple assertion with "Of course you have an imagination."

He was steadfast. "No! I don't!"

His crying continued. I asked him to take a deep breath and started posing some of those simple questions that typically trigger long narratives from children: Each of my questions was met with more tears and a series of stern admonitions. "I don't know!"

His frustration was thick as fog. Clearly it was time for a different approach.

Some students are not at ease with creating written language. Many of these young people are much more comfortable in the world of numbers, data, and facts. The language of numbers or the world of science may be more intrinsic to their processing or their interests. Others are great oral storytellers or illustrators, but are loath to render their tales in writing or simply too impatient to translate the images flying about in their heads onto the paper before them, their hands lagging far behind the rapid pace of their ideas. This time lag is also a factor of the 21st Century, where more and more children are being referred to as "digital natives" in the media. Just the time it takes to use a pen or pencil to capture thoughts may contribute to reticence. Often, if students can use a keyboard, they will be more willing to write, as well as more productive.

This appeared to be a teaching situation in which Howard Gardner's theory of multiple intelligences, the different ways that the human brain is able to learn, would become evident. As Gardner outlined, there are different learning styles by which we collect and retain knowledge; therefore, by incorporating different elements in the learning process, more students are likely to connect with the material through their individual methods of processing. I have come to understand that by bringing logic, visual art, dance, recitation, even number recognition in some activities, into my practice, I develop deeper points of entry with students. To test my understanding in practical application, I asked this young man if he was more comfortable with the language of numbers, if math is easy for him. He looked up and the tears stopped. "Yes," he nearly whispered. Oh! Great! We had found a starting point!

I continued, "Well, I can't speak that language well at all! I will make you a deal. You make up a math quiz tonight for me to do tomorrow and I will help you with this." Now we had a connection. We made a pact. There was hope for us both. We flipped through the pictures in the books he had checked out from the library for his refresher. I asked more questions. One illustration showed cartoon penguins sliding down ice into water on their bellies. Well, there is a lot a kid can do that resembles that image! *Have you ever been to a water park? Have you ever been sledding on a big hill or used just your belly to slide in the snow?* Once the student started making connections and his tears dried, my last step was to ask his fellow students in the adjacent desks to help this boy, since they were all nearly done with their first drafts. They agreed, with obvious compassion and generosity of spirit, and I left to attend to other students. Before I left for another class, I reminded my penguin that I would be looking for my quiz the next morning, and I asked him to be tough on me. He smiled broadly.

When I arrived in the classroom the next day, my day-four lesson plan was to facilitate a peer-to-peer review of the draft persona poems from the previous session, and to ask the writers to revise their poems based on peer critique while working in small groups. I stopped by to see my math whiz and ask if I had a number puzzle to solve. Although he sheepishly said no, he was smiling. I moved on with my lesson. The different islands of students were engaged in workshopping their poems, all reflecting the research and discussion from earlier in the week. I was a proud poet, seeing all these young writers building skills together, discussing form, structure, synonym choices, challenging and affirming one another. When I happened past my penguin in discussion with the rest of his menagerie, he was ardently posing a recommendation of form and grammar that was surprising—and perfect—to improve his friend's poem. He had taken in so much more than I realized of the poetic elements I had illustrated early in the week with "Bear Song." Wow! All of the animals were taking form and poems were happening. What a treat.

Before I left that fourth day, I stopped by my new friend's desk for a moment to ask him a simple question or two. "Why do you think you might be able to make up a math quiz for me? How would you just invent problems for me to solve?"

He looked at me for a moment and responded very quietly, "My imagination?"

"Absolutely! Just because the way I think is easy for me and the way you think is easy for you does not mean that one of us has more imagination than another. We just use ours differently. That's all."

The next day, my last with this group, I issued one more request for my quiz and received the same sheepish smile. Although he had not prepared a math test for me, the fact that I asked for it created a trust that continued to keep this young man striving to meet my expectations.

I am never sure how the magic of creating art with language happens. I believe that it has a lot to do with the fact that all children will allow, at some point, suspension of the belief that they are incapable of meeting the task at hand, no matter what that task may be. Children now seem very concerned with two questions: *Is this done?* and *Is this good?* It is imperative to urge them to reach past simply being *done* into a depth of awareness from which to address the question, *And then what?*

We must connect with students as authentically as possible to affirm that they are creative, sentient beings with tremendous capacity to amaze others; to remind them that their visions and opinions matter. It is possible for each of us to realize that we have the capacity to change minds through the power of language. We can make others see what we see, believe what we believe; words make that possible, if we can use them effectively. Language is the tool of both empathy and change. Teach a child this and she just may make her way through the world successfully. Remind an adult and he will be equally affirmed.

We arrived at our sharing day, my chance to witness 25 acts of magic. We had cheetahs and sharks, dolphins and dogs, ferrets and pandas all in one room, telling their tales in verse. My penguin stood when it was his turn. I stood near him in case he needed support. I noticed his paper was filled with neatly revised, tight couplets, just as "Bear Song" is structured.

He slid on his belly into the bitterly cold water. He spoke of his family and his mother's long journey to the sea, his favorite breakfast fish. He was on an iceberg at the South Pole, speaking in another language, and it was beautiful.

HAVE CAMERA, WILL TRAVEL

Georgia A. Popoff

When I made the decision to pursue teaching artistry as full-time employment, I recognized the need for a cell phone upgrade, a new computer, and a sturdy yet small digital camera. I went out on a limb to invest in the equipment. It took one teaching week to confirm that I made a wise decision. The camera is the best of the three tools for accommodating countless needs. I have been able to appease restless students in various grade levels with trips around the school grounds or hallways taking pictures and then writing from the visual prompts. I have been able to snap photos of all of my blackboard notes at the end of each class so I can document my processes and compare notes.

I have also used the camera to work with self-contained special-education classes creating self-reflective portraits—a lesson meant to strengthen skills regarding parts of speech. This process led to a unique and unexpected outcome for one group of students with special learning needs. I met this small group of sixth-graders in an ELA class in the morning, only to discover that I was to work with them again in their afternoon literacy class. I had not planned a second lesson for the day. As I improvised, I asked the class, six boys, to list three adjectives they thought best described them. Then, since they were all very good friends, I asked them to describe each other with a single adjective as I made lists for each student. The next step was to take these lists and write "I Am..." statements using each adjective in a separate sentence. This was the effort for day two.

On day three, we took on the roles of portrait photographers. I showed the boys how my camera worked. They staged shots of themselves and each other posing in a manner that would best depict the "I Am" statements from the day before. I also took group shots of the band of buddies. That evening, using my computer, I designed a personalized template for each of them that had one or two portraits of them individually, along with a group shot. I gave each a title of "I Am..." followed by their first names. Then I created a text box with lines so they could transcribe their word portraits onto the form. The next day, I printed the pages off in the computer lab before school and distributed them in class. The resultant laughter was joyous.

The first project in which I incorporated digital technology was an after-school poetry video interpretation of *I Am America*, a gem of a picture book on diversity by photographer and writer, Charles R. Smith Jr. At the prompting of my co-teacher, the school's resourceful library/media specialist, we entered a contest sponsored by Syracuse University to interpret one of four books by Smith using some digital device. Our fourth-graders made a collaborative video poem modeled on the book's general theme. First we wrote individual poems on the theme, then we used a line or two from each poem for the group piece. The students translated their poems into Word documents with clip art to strengthen computer skills and further interpret their own work. Then my colleague taught them how to use a video camera and they set about directing their poem in a video. Some of the children learned to edit as well. The video won first prize. The school was awarded a new laptop for the library and the kids attended a presentation with Charles and an awards luncheon. Best of all, they got out of school for a day for the field trip. And I was hooked!

I have participated in numerous projects that mix digital images into the plan. I access Google Maps to illustrate a bird's-eye view to accompany a poem. I love the computer lab, a great place to provoke poetry.

One of my favorite projects spanned two years at Maple Hill Elementary School in Middletown, New York, in partnership with the Children's Media Project (CMP) of Poughkeepsie. The project required a major investment by the school district to match the funds provided by a New York State Council on the Arts' Empire State Partnership program grant we had been awarded. An arts-integrated learning unit was designed that would involve three classes of fourth-grade English language learners creating persona poems based on animals they chose from science study. Then the children would work with CMP staff to learn to use video cameras and to film each other acting their poems, as had the fourth-graders from the project upstate years before. Three classes, 25 students each, five days to generate 75 poems that would be ready to shoot. The video portion of the project would also need to be completed in five days. Ten days total with approximately six teaching artists in two media and five teachers to create all of the video poems from introduction to final edit. We did it! The students were delighted, many parents came to school for a screening, everybody was happy. The teaching artists were all exhausted, and we made a commitment to finding a way to work smarter, not harder.

The next year we would concentrate on the power of collaboration while retaining the successful elements from year one. Once again, poems would be developed by three classes of fourth-grade English language learners. I would use the model of the previous award-winning project incorporating the same theme and book I had relied upon in the after-school project. Since this was a book on diversity, it made sense to structure the project around that topic, given that we were working with students for whom English was a second language and whose families were adapting to life in the United States.

Each of the three classes had different levels of English-language proficiency and this was a terrific way not only to support literacy skills but also to honor all of the students and their many heritages. To build on what we developed the prior year, we designed the second-year program to include the students from the previous year. The project unfolded in this manner:

- Again we had 10 days, five of which were for me to create poems with the classes, first individual poems and then a collaborative piece for each class, three final poems total to be animated by the fifth-graders.

- The fifth-graders who were part of the project the year before would once again work with CMP to interpret the poems, again in five days but this time in stop-action animation. Three classes, one poem per class. The art faculty was also involved to help storyboard and create the images, as well as film them.

- The poems examined and celebrated the diversity of the classrooms, with the premise that we are all Americans.

To start the writing process, it was first necessary to determine the depth of diversity among the participants. A poll of the students, class by class, to trace heritage and original nationalities provided a profile of the multinational demographic of this school. Each class developed a series of interview questions that students would use as homework to find more details about lineage and the lives of their parents and grandparents, all of which went into our central "database" for composing the poems. These questions for family members included:

- Where did you [your parents or grandparents] meet?

- What was school like when you were my age?

- What was the house you grew up in like?

- What was your favorite food or game to play when you were young?

- When you were young, what was your favorite holiday and how did you celebrate it?

I suggested that the students explain to their parents that this survey was for a poetry project since there may have been sensitivities about sharing this information. Some of these families are undocumented residents and I did not want them to think that we were using their children to gain information about their residency status.

We also developed a personal survey for students to answer, presented as "questions that tell surprises about ourselves," all of which could then be turned into "I am" statements:

- Where is my family from?

- What is something that I like to do that my parents also liked to do when they were my age?

- What is my favorite color? Why?

- What is my favorite season of the year? Why?

- What is my favorite food to eat? Why?

- What is my favorite book or author? Why?

- When I sleep, do I dream? What are my dreams about?

- What do I hope to be when I am an adult?

- Who do I know who shares my dreams for my future?

- Do I look like my mother, my father, or both?

- What is my special talent?

The results were remarkable. The students outlined similarities and commonalities among themselves: favorite foods, music, clothes, activities, books, etc. They mentioned their dreams for the future and their sleeping dreams. The lists were magical and raw, perfect fodder for the construction of poetry. The rule in fabricating the imagery was simple: if more than one person had the same response, then the statement was to be in terms of the collective "we." Unique responses were "I" statements. We collaborated to determine language choices, as each class developed a slightly different process. We maintained the same keen writing skills and process that we were using for the individual poems. We revised to develop similes and metaphors that would translate into visual images for the video. A great deal can be illustrated in single images that transcend language. Because voice-overs of the poems were to be recorded, the music of the words was imperative.

The animation process had its constraints but making three videos instead of 75 made the process much easier than the previous year, yet still met all of the objectives of providing a multi-layered and meaningful learning experience that crossed cultures, core subject areas, and skill sets. The fifth-graders worked in collaborative groups to interpret the poems, brainstorm images, storyboard their films, make the pieces they would need to record, and then do the videotaping. They quickly remembered how to use the camera after a short refresher.

Five days later, after a lot of adult elbow grease, the animations were completed. Once again, parents, teachers, students, artists, funders, and district representatives were all delighted. The work is touching and humorous with a poignant flair that cannot be manufactured. Here's one of the poems, a poem that forges language into a concrete statement of unity peppered with ample opportunity for the visual.

We are.....................I am

We are Mexico
I am Honduras
I am India
I am Egypt
We are Puerto Rican
We are American

We are ciudadanos..............I am an immigrant

We are blue as the clear sky, melting icicles and deep oceans
I am red as hot lava bursting from an erupting volcano
I am yellow as lemony gum

We are a rainbow...............I am a color

We are breakdancing Hip-Hop
I am gospel at church
I am soothing Jazz
We are rhyming Rap

We are music...............I am a song

We are sweaty basketball jerseys at Madison Square Garden
I am shorts and sandals on a tropical island
I am a soft, blue bandanna on a farm

We are new.................I am worn

We are The Lion, The Witch, and The Wardrobe
I am C.S. Lewis
I am Goosebumps
We are fiction, mysteries, and biographies

We are readers...............I am an author

We hope to be a police officer on a SWAT team
I hope to be a rich and famous baseball player
I hope to be a biologist
We hope to be teachers

We are a job............I am a worker

We dream that we are skateboarders and wonderful teachers
I dream that monkeys are chasing me
I dream about eating at Chucky Cheese

We are dreamers...........I am a child

We share this dream with our families
I share this dream with my mom, dad, brothers, and sisters
I share this dream with no one, I keep it a secret

We share our thoughts........I share my imagination

—Mrs. Sgandurra's fourth-grade class,
2008,
Maple Hill Elementary School,
Middletown, New York

COMPREHENSIVE LESSON PLAN

Five-Day Persona Poems

Georgia A. Popoff

Objective: To engage students in utilizing research to create poems that reflect knowledge in core content areas other than English language arts, while also enhancing study skills, general literacy, writing competency, and reading comprehension.

> **Applicable Age/Grade Level:** Applicable to any age group or grade level, modifying to accommodate literacy, writing, and research skills.
>
> **Anticipated Time:** This lesson is best suited to a week-long (five-day) process.
>
> **Materials/Resources Needed:** Writing materials (paper, pen/pencil), dictionary, thesaurus, access to the library and computer labs.

Process Overview:
Persona poems are wonderful vehicles that allow students to demonstrate their knowledge about history, science, or literature by writing in the voice and with the perspective of others. As such, these poems are particularly useful for writing in a cross-disciplinary context and teaching strategies can be easily adapted for use across the curriculum.

Day One–Initiating the Discussion:
Day one is a general introduction and overview in which the teacher presents a selected theme related to a core content area, preferably one that has already been studied. For example, the class may have read about the South American rainforest and the mammals, reptiles, amphibians, birds, fish, and insects that live there. (Other options could include an historical figure, a noted mathematician or scientist, a character from literature, or

even inanimate objects being studied in other content areas.) Ask each student to choose a rainforest animal to identify with in order write a poem in the voice of their choice.

Discuss with the students how we, as humans, have the capacity to empathize with others and why details from research will be critical in understanding and speaking in the voice of the animals they've chosen

Day Two–Moving into the Writing Component:

Day two involves engaging students in fact finding, the first key to student success in this project. Create a set of questions for students to use in searching for details needed to imagine and create a character's voice as if it were their own. Questions that can generate ideas for the creative writing process include:

- Where did you wake up?
- When did you wake up? Are you nocturnal?
- What did you eat for breakfast and how/where do you get your food?
- If you see your reflection, what do you look like?
- Do you live alone or with others?
- What is your family like?
- How would you describe the place you live?
- What does your voice sound like?
- How do you travel?
- What size are you?
- How long do you live?
- How do you feel today?
- What does the world around you look like?
- What sounds surround you in your habitat?

This fact-finding work may be done in the library, the computer lab, or the classroom—wherever needed resources are available to students.

Day Three–Drafting the Poem:

Day three's discussion builds on the notes students took during their research. Ask students to respond to the previous day's questions, sharing their ideas with the whole class. Remind the students to respond in the first person, as if they have "morphed" into their characters. The goal is to tell the tale that the animals would relate to someone who does not know about them. This must be reinforced a great deal or there will be too much data; the writing will be too literal. Prompting from the list of questions and following their responses to a chosen line of inquiry with the simple question, "And then what happened?" will expand the scope of nearly every student's response. Allow free writing time for students to develop a draft poem of at least 12 lines.

Day Four–Revising for Success:

On day four, ask students to review what they have written thus far, considering all the aspects of quality writing (e.g., word choice, simile and metaphor, descriptive language, active verbs). Emphasize the importance of verb and adjective choice. Provide 10 to15 minutes to make changes. Remind students to think in terms of figurative language.

Divide the students into groups of three or four or have them work in pairs to share and critique each other's drafts. Ask them to look for typos, misspelled words, grammatical errors, and improper punctuation, in addition to responding to the poem's content. Remind students that critique is not criticism. Encourage the "sandwich" method of critique: offer a positive comment, a suggestion for improvement, and another positive comment.

Day Five–Finalizing the Draft:

On day five, give students 5 to 10 minutes to proofread their work one more time. Then have them type and print or handwrite the final copy.

Also on day five, have students share their work with the class by reading it aloud and allowing others to respond. If there is someone who is reticent to share, ask the student if someone else, including yourself, can read the piece for them. It can be very affirming to hear a teacher read a student's work out loud, just as seeing their work typed can instill a sense of pride and encourage effort. If there is time in the sharing/performance aspect of the final day, allow students to offer further critique of each other's poems.

Expected Outcomes:

- Assessment of learning and retention from units of study in other core content areas.

- Development of research methods and skills, creative problem-solving, critical thinking, and empathy.

- Students will support each other in learning, sharing ideas and concepts, and strengthening writing skills.

- Continued skill enhancement in English language arts.

COMPREHENSIVE LESSON PLAN

Baseball Game Persona Poems

Georgia A. Popoff & Quraysh Ali Lansana

Objectives: To induce creative imagining, role play, and inference, in addition to critical thinking and identifying contextual clues. Knowledge of particular historical figures or characters from literature will be increased through research. Developing a story line in a poem will be emphasized.

Applicable Age/Grade level: This lesson is adaptable to all grade levels, modified by skill set and level of maturity.

Anticipated Time: Adaptable from one class session to a five-day exercise.

Materials/Resources Needed: Writing materials (paper, pen/pencil), dictionary, thesaurus, access to the library and computer labs.

Process Overview:

In this twist on the Five-Day Persona Poems lesson, students write persona poems that place their characters in unexpected settings. Students not only need to conduct research to learn about their characters, they also must make an imaginative leap to describe the character in a new experience, such as Marie Curie at Yankee Stadium.

Initiating the Discussion:

Ask students to brainstorm historical figures or fictional characters they find interesting and list those names on the board. This is an opportunity to emphasize individuals from the curriculum units you are currently studying in social studies, the sciences, and literature. Invite students to imagine arbitrary situations from life today, such as a baseball game or a concert, and list those on the board as well. Lead students in a discussion about what one of the noted characters from history or literature might say or how she might feel if she found herself in the bleachers at that game or the nosebleed seats at the concert.

Moving into the Writing Component:

Ask students to create persona poems in the voice of that historical figure or fictional character, and in the contemporary setting of their choice. Employing the scenario below, start to brainstorm responses with your students. Record these responses for future reference, using whatever medium is available in the classroom.

Modeling for Poetic Structure:

Set up a scenario for the students, such as: *You will be writing in the voice of Marie Curie. It is opening day at Yankee Stadium. Madame Curie has a box seat. Give her a voice, not in dialogue with another character, but through her response to being a fish out of water. Your poem will essentially be the character's interior dialogue. Think about the following questions as you develop your poems:*

- What time of day is it?

- Who else is in the box?

- What was Madame Curie doing an hour ago?

- How did she arrive at the stadium?

- What snack/refreshment does she select?

- What questions does she have at this moment?

- What will she do after the game?

The answers to these questions develop a platform for the first draft. Other noted figures to consider may include any of the following from history, science, literature, mythology or popular culture: John Brown, Icarus, Kanye West, Donald Trump, Genghis Khan, Jay Gatsby, Hugo Chavez, Coretta Scott King. You may even ask students to think more abstractly to develop a voice for a paramecium, a glacier, a particular number—anything that presses them into creative and imaginative thought.

Drafting the Poem:

Prompt students using the list of questions above, as well as your own. Following their oral responses to a chosen line of inquiry, encourage students to delve further into character development with the simple question, "And then what happened?" to expand the response. Allow for free writing time to develop a draft poem of at least 12 lines.

Revising for Success:

Divide the students into groups of three or four or have them work in pairs to share their drafts and critique and support each other. Ask students to note typos, misspelled words, grammatical errors, and improper punctuation, as well as commenting on the content of the poem. Remind them that critique is not criticism. Encourage the "sandwich" method of critique: offer a positive comment, a suggestion for improvement, and another positive comment.

Publishing and Performance:

Have students share their work with the class and allow the class to respond. If there is someone who is reticent in sharing, ask the student if someone else, including yourself, can read the piece aloud. It can be very affirming to hear a teacher read a student's work out loud, just as seeing their work typed can instill a sense of pride and encourage effort. If there is time in the sharing/performance aspect of the final day, allow for further critique. Other performance opportunities, such as a poetry café, school assembly, or gathering for parents may be considered. Still another possibility is to establish a "museum" in which the characters are presented in various forms (e.g., students dress as their characters and perform the poems or create poster boards with background information).

Expected Outcomes:

- Further knowledge of the subject, character, or unit of study selected to provide the foundation for the poems written.

- Strengthened language-arts knowledge and communication skills, along with empathy and critical thinking.

- General English-language-arts skill sets strengthened.

- Research skills and methods enhanced.

- Further assessment of knowledge retention from prior units of study.

POETRY AND DIVERSITY

Language, Emotion, and Shared Experience

INTRODUCTION

Georgia A. Popoff & Quraysh Ali Lansana

> Once the poet was our spokesman and not
> our oracle, our advocate and not our secret
> agent, or at least he or she was as much the
> one as the other; and if the poet did not
> speak for us, all of us, fully and warmly, if
> the poems lacked the larger vision of
> humanity, we said he or she was deficient in
> one of the qualities which, virtually by
> definition, make a poet.
>   —Hayden Carruth, "Poets Without Prophecy"

There is a notion that most folks form the foundations for interaction with one another within the first 11 seconds of meeting; humans develop their opinions about the value of others in that short time span. Consider this reality within the crucible of a middle-school classroom in any small working-class town experiencing rapid and unexpected changes in the ethnic makeup of the community, due to the great expense of living in the nearby big city. School (and town) may now breed tensions directly connected to race and class.

It seems that humans have an inherent need to elevate themselves by denigrating others. Cliques and factions become human attributes. Allow us to view the changing face of contemporary society: for instance, any small American city with a history of agriculture and manufacturing that transforms into a suburban bedroom community, then evolves into a location for people of lower socio-economic means to find affordable housing. This creates a recipe for resentment and polarization.

Additionally, we may find many nationalities lumped into one neighborhood, thereby creating a second tier of polarization based on national chauvinism (e.g., I'm not Mexican, I'm Colombian; I'm not African American, I'm Jamaican). Rooted in displacement, preserving heritage is an obvious by-product of a society based upon a history of colonization and migration. Including the shrouded history of what remains of the indigenous peoples of North America, the American populace is haunted by leaving home behind or being ripped from it unwillingly. This pattern of movement even plays out throughout US history in the development of the western territories in the 1800s, the northern urban centers throughout the 20th Century, and the recent migrations of refugees from Asia and Eastern Europe, from throughout Africa, from Haiti, Cuba, South and Central America. In every case, families are rent apart and the need to cling to their lineage becomes more pressing.

These are difficult times. The rapidly changing climate of public-school classrooms presents new challenges to educators. Additional obstacles facing students and teachers alike include:

- International economic recession;

- Violence evident in schools and communities;

- Societal traumas that render our youth victims of stress and illness often left unrecognized; and

- Natural disasters that destroy whole cities, depleting the citizenry.

A single classroom may include English language learners, students on the autism spectrum, a range of socio-economic classes, children from split or single-parent homes, students familiar with domestic abuse, and young people immersed in communities rife with street violence. How do we possibly address all of these concerns in public schools successfully? Classroom teachers must be adequately prepared to cope with a 13-year-old who has spent his early stages of life in the refugee camps of Africa or the conflicts of Eastern Europe. They may have to accommodate the brunt of trauma such as September 11th or Hurricane Katrina on the hearts of our youth. In the face of the 2010 earthquake, schools must effectively support students of Haitian descent whose relatives were left behind.

Is there a method to teach daily lesson plans to young people who have witnessed mass shootings in their schools, while adequately exhibiting concern for their tender spots? Are educators prepared with sufficient cultural reference to honor the young woman who has just taken the hijab, or to develop adequate empathy to support the child whose parent is unknown? A young person's behavioral problems may relate to a sense of hopelessness and alienation; teachers are often the first to recognize these symptoms. Through a teacher's concern for students, negative behaviors may be seen as evidence of difficulty rather than punishable offenses. Our house of education must create a safe space for dialogue regarding any of the emotional and social issues, among either faculty or students themselves.

If the educational system is possibly failing to provide the training and expertise necessary to meet the ever-changing needs of the faces in our schools, how is the overall learning environment impacted? How are both student and teacher affected? Moreover, as citizens who must share this nation, how are we encouraged to speak, understand, and accept people who are different from us, yet who face similar privileges and problems? How can we possibly support the notion of a post-racial America in the context of this reality of difference and conflict, rooted in generations of fear and loss? As teachers walk into their classrooms 180 days per year, these questions fuel the undercurrent of their own work. These same concerns impel our conviction that poetry is a valuable tool not just for learning, but also for awareness and acceptance of diversity and similarities.

A teacher will find catalysts to spark meaningful dialogue among students by cultivating a repository of poetry beyond the classic examples that have guided the canon of English language arts instruction for many years. We recognize similarities among each of us, expressed in unique cultural and familial ways, through teaching a poem such as "Knoxville, Tennessee," by Nikki Giovanni, or Li-Young Lee's "Early in the Morning." These poets, among countless others, allow readers to peer through windows into family ritual and relationship that show not just how different our families may be, but how similar the human condition is, no matter our background, skin tone, or geography.

A diverse sampling of established writers will provide models to initiate students' own poetic statements, giving voice to their particular circumstance. Contemporary poets such as Patrick Rosal, Kwame Dawes,

Joy Harjo, Kimiko Hahn, Debra Kang Dean, Martha Collins, and Reginald Gibbons will each provide portraits of American life that illustrate many shadings of one race, human.

In the effort to afford students access to poetic voices from diverse backgrounds, we recognize that there is an inherent roadblock that may also amplify a concern teachers have expressed to both of us many times. Teachers are often unfamiliar, even uncomfortable, with teaching poetry. In fact, it is this impediment and the call for assistance from classroom educators that have directed us to articulate our perspective.

As poets, we are expressing a form of outreach with each school we visit and within these pages. By proposing a diversity of examples beyond the textbooks available to a teacher, we do not anticipate, nor require, that the teacher be well-versed in the nuance of all world cultures in order to teach poems from diverse eras and places. It may actually be more of a collaborative achievement for a teacher and students to investigate a poem together and question each other in ways that build trust and empathy, as well as allowing teachers to model lifelong learning.

As teaching writers, those 11-second first impressions may enable our success within the learning environment and thwart the limitations of time afforded us in our periods of residency.

As teaching artists, we probably suffer as much as we benefit by being visitors to the classroom. We expect to learn as much from our students as we attempt to offer and as we hope they learn from us. We enter each class openly and with respect for both student and teacher. We know that we are asking for immediate trust and respect, as well as a considerable commitment on behalf of each class to work with us within the extreme time constraints of the typical writer's residency. We also understand that we ask a great deal of each of our host teachers as they invite us into their learning spaces. We take up their instruction time, we change their routines, we need some of the precious supplies that they likely purchased with money from their own pockets.

The ideas presented in this section's essays emanated from within the American ideal of the national melting pot, which we were taught to honor as we grew up. The processes of inquiry that this section presents were experienced in classes comprised predominantly of young people of color, but they are applicable in any circumstance. We teach from a platform based on the dynamics of our individual backgrounds, coupled with the celebration of diversity. Our platform declares that poetry is a vehicle by which we all can enthusiastically celebrate our differences as well as commonalities as citizens and humans. The essays examine attitudes, cultural and political influences, and some ways in which young people access language. They reflect how our youth are faced with pressing issues regarding identity and some manners in which these pressures manifest. We also acknowledge potential constraints of the typical writing residency, including limited planning time and days in the classroom, and short instructional periods.

During our residencies, students may identify a place within themselves to express their own creativity and self-awareness through the avenue of poetry. Additionally, we hope to foster a willingness to listen to and respect others. The ultimate goal is that young people will strengthen their sense of oneness and community, rather than fearing differences, by giving voice to their truths, as well as honoring the voices of others through reading and writing.

NAME CALLING: THE LANGUAGE OF THE STREETS

Quraysh Ali Lansana

In February 2008, Primary Election Day, a brooding Chicago morning, my oldest son, Nile, and I waved my other school-aged son, Onam, off to school and walked the long South Side block to my Jeep. There was little to settle Nile's anxiety. A prolific writer and true bibliophile, missing a day of school was a serious thing to Nile. His trepidation about the day centered on the task that lay before him behind dingy, blonde brick on the corner of 51st and State Street. Nile was about to undergo three hours of testing for admission to one of the gifted and talented magnet programs of the Chicago Public Schools. He actually initiated his academic career at one of these schools, one that touted the highest test scores in the state. But the price was too high. The volume of work was so great and the pressure on my son so heavy, I moved him to a private school after kindergarten.

Nile only agreed to the tests because he hated our neighborhood with as much vigor as he consumes books. Our block was a *Fox News* playland. Drugs, gangs, kitchen chairs holding parking spots in the street on snow days, and working-class people trying to clear a better path. It made Nile uneasy. It made me uneasy too, raising four Black boys in this grim reality. He knew we couldn't afford a new house in a safer neighborhood *and* private school tuition, even with scholarships. Teaching my sons to love themselves, and their culture, while dodging bullets is challenging work.

To that end, there's another public education curriculum to consider. Nile and Onam spent two months at a city park summer camp, then broke up with Hannah Montana because Lil Wayne didn't think she had enough junk in her trunk; Lil Wayne, author of the following uplifting lyrics:

> (Yeahh)... Doin a buck in the latest drop
> I got stopped by a lady cop
> Ha Ha... she got me thinking I can date a cop
> Ha Ha... cause her uniform pants are so tight
> She read me my rights

She put me in the car, she cut off all the lights
She said I had the right to remain silent
Now I got her hollering sounding like a siren
Talkin' bout...
Wee Ooh Wee Ooh Wee (Yea)

—Lil Wayne (Dwayne Carter),
"Mrs. Officer"

Lil Wayne is capable of brilliant poetry, if he would just use his powers for good. But it's not just him. The endless barrage of commercial literature, television, and video games are just as damning as commercial radio. This is the reservoir from which most young people, certainly most Black and Brown teenagers drink, the lens through which they see themselves. This is youth culture, as defined by whom? Beyoncé/Sasha Fierce? While she is supporting monogamy and marriage in "Single Ladies (Put a Ring on It)," in the song's video she's half-naked and dances as if someone is giving her a spanking. Even I am confused. But when your nine-year-old son begins singing Lil Wayne lyrics from the back of the mini-van, you search for clarity very quickly.

Teachers and teaching artists must nurture classrooms that support our students' capacities to create change in the immediate, as well as the future. We live in desperate times. We are losing too many young people. Armed with new ways of challenging the norms, we can offer the notion of involvement toward change as opposed to a continued endorsement of the status quo. Through exploration of the written word as a conduit for self-knowledge and shared understanding, we can guide our students to examine current trends and ideas, thus challenging them to find ways to create change. It is in our hands to create this imperative, to open young eyes to their own relevance and cast concrete steps to take in building the kind of world in which they and their children wish to live.

As educators, we must find a way to keep language compelling while endorsing the notion that this commercial collective voice is not the defining one. What methods must we devise to redirect the energies of young people who live the language of the streets, while at the same time acknowledging the needs of youngsters like Nile and Onam who have accessed this language because it is the tongue of their *Now*? How do we open dialogues that reflect our respect for the uniqueness of the culture in which our youth are immersed, while rejecting the values of which pop culture so often speaks?

In 2001, Michael Powell was appointed chairman of the Federal Communications Commission (FCC). During his tenure, Powell deregulated the airwaves to allow space for the *n-word* and the *b-word* on commercial, prime-time media, driven in part by the buying power of 15- to 25-year olds. This decision opened the floodgates to profanity on the air. In an attempt to minimize the frequency of obscenities broadcast on live radio and television, the FCC applied to the US Court of Appeals for the Second Circuit in Manhattan to enforce stronger language restrictions. In July 2010, the court ruled this application unconstitutional, giving greater lenience to broadcast media.

How many of us over 40 years of age could have imagined *bitch* falling from Eva Longoria's lips on the TV show *Desperate Housewives'* Wisteria Lane on a Sunday night? The last three decades of urban or urban-inspired youth culture, as reflected in Hip Hop, have done more than simply claim the words *bitch* and *nigga*. They have redefined them. *Bitch* may have replaced *BFF* as a girl's familial term for her closest female friend. Additionally, as proclaimed by rapper Lil' Kim, *bitch* might be considered a power word or a term for a woman who is in control. There appears to be a gender bias regarding this term, however. There are rare occasions that a young man can directly refer to a young woman as such and not have it be perceived as insult. However, it is quite ordinary and acceptable to hear male Hip-Hop, Rap, or R&B stars call women *bitch* every other nanosecond via a very supportive media machine. Might it be that the rapper is referring to some other woman? Comedian Katt Williams, in one of his stand-up routines, said "I'm only calling you bitches because I don't know your names individually." I assume the reader is familiar with the textbook definition.

One of the aspects of the *b-word* that is deeply unnerving is the possibility, if not the likelihood, that there are at least three generations of young women for whom the term is as common as a pronoun or the body's need for water. *Bitch* has become as self-referential as one's name. We've all suffered through rote learning.

Nigga is on an even heavier rotation than the *b-word* and has become so pervasive members of non-African-American ethnic groups refer to themselves as such. Only watching 20-something White liberals stumble over its moment in the hook of Kanye West's "Golddigger" is as oddly fascinating as hearing it spit by teenage White boys anywhere.

A few years ago, Georgia and I were conducting a professional development workshop for teaching artists and high school teachers in Detroit. We were invited to a reading in a predominantly Mexican neighborhood, and as soon as we stepped out of our host's car we heard *nigga, nigga, nigga, nigga* mixed with Spanish and thick accents. As they gathered in the front yard of a house on the block, the group of 20- to 30-year-old men was not talking to or about me. They were simply engrossed in conversation. I was dumbstruck.

Yet, with the renaissance of the blatant usage of the *n-word*, a White man can still not call a Black man *nigger* without swift and immediate repercussions. Many books have been written on the word in recent years, as well as a revival surrounding the debate of its usage and ownership. I won't extrapolate here; the point is if it's not okay for a White man to call a Black man *nigger*, what makes it okay for a Black man to call another Black man, or Latino/Chicano man, *nigga?* In what laboratory was the notion cooked that *nigga* could be self-referential for non-Black people? Is Hip-Hop/Rap music to blame?

That *nigger/nigga* plays such a significant role in the vernacular of our young people at this time is compounded by the reality that the US has elected the first African-American president. The rhetoric behind much of the organized opposition to the Obama Administration is laced with racial hatred. "Let's take our country back!" From whom? Native Americans might have a few things to share on this topic. "Heritage Not Hate" blazes on Ku-Klux-Klan billboards as their membership swells. And I'm certain the language of the unorganized opposition to President Obama is not fit to print.

Nigger/nigga and *bitch,* though both spoken and heard every day and night, remain complicated terms, despite their appearance on high-frequency lists. They are "push-button words" for many people, young and old, of all ethnicities. I, too, have a troubled and convoluted history with the *n-word*. In third grade, I beat up a kid who called me *nigger*. My father used the word to dress down Black men who were not taking care of their responsibilities, but rarely uttered it around the family.

While working in Michigan with eighth-graders from various middle schools, I led a discussion about these two words, as much for myself as the students. The poem below captures my many thoughts and emotions based on the conversations among the participants in the workshop.

eighth grade

I.

teens in kalamazoo tell me
words that spark indifference:
nigger (note spelling), bitch,
hoe (note spelling), then confirm
emcee's spat those lyrics at them
that week, that morning

II.

the n-word slouches with phonics:
er is insult, *a* is family. Only
marshall mathers & other
bi-racial people can drop
nig*ga* and not get beat down

III.

a nervous young man, who loves
rap, shows me his essay in confidence,
declines to read it to the class
they won't understand, they'll tease me
feels white boy is as bad as nigger

in the mouth of the beholder

IV.

it means *female dog* and since she is not
she can endure the gathering
of hooded nike super-heroes
who meet on fabulous corners
to consider every woman but her

she, herself also super, possesses
the ability to separate beat from lyric,
is certain fifty took all nine bullets,
of michael jackson's guilt, tupac's breath

After students uncovered the word or phrase that made them fighting mad, I asked them to write about the associative memories or issues from their lives, the context. I followed that by guiding students to write about how they diffuse the words' mass destructiveness. In another workshop, in Syracuse, New York, an African-American young man told me, through tears, his push-button phrase was *You ain't neva gonna be shit*, administered daily by his mother. His plan to diffuse its impact was to graduate from high school, go to college, and be successful. My hope is he proved his mother wrong, but the interior devastation of that phrase is not a quick fix, not an Oprah moment. It may take his entire lifetime to overcome the poison of those words.

After Nile completed his tests, he slumped through the doorway. I stood to hug him. Coats on, we lifted our heavy weights—his backpack and my briefcase—both with too many books, then headed to the Jeep for our next stop. Neither of us ever travels far without reading material and journal. On the way we talked about Sasha and Malia's daddy, about when our team last played Malia's team in September (Nile and Onam played; I coached). How two soccer dads barked encouragement from opposing sidelines, and that the dudes with things in their ears were there because of death threats. Not the kind that come with gangsta bravado and back-beat.

In the dimly lit church basement, Nile drew the curtain around us in the booth. "Can I do it, Dad?" he asked. "Can I punch Number 1?"

THE SOFT BIGOTRY OF DIMINISHED EXPECTATIONS

Georgia A. Popoff

> Given the pressures on children in schools to factualize
> the world, to maintain a homogenized standard of
> thought, a poetic way of perceiving experience is simply
> ignored as an indulgence. There is, in the increasingly
> test-driven curriculum, little time for it. Still, I have
> found in my work with children that if we do pay
> attention to this poetic ability there is a dramatic shift
> in children's sense of themselves and their desire to
> learn. By affirming their poetic ability we open up a
> natural instinct in children to bring the outer world
> into the inner world of themselves—to link the
> phenomena of the world, in all its complexity, to the
> phenomena of one's self.
> —Richard Lewis, *Taking Flight, Standing Still:*
> *Teaching Toward Poetic and Imaginative*
> *Understanding*

Several years ago, I taught in an inner-city middle school where, sadly, gunfire in the neighborhood is much too prevalent. Early in the class period, while preparing the students to brainstorm for their writing project, a district supply truck was loading furniture and materials into the school. From a couple of floors below the window, a sharp noise bit the morning air, startling the class. One young man immediately ducked and starting scanning the room, his jacket pulled over his head, peering past his collar. The noise echoed that of a gunshot and the student did as he is always prepared to do—drop and protect himself. He quickly realized the sound was benign. As he laughed at himself a bit, I caught his eye. He straightened his body and took his chair. I smiled and quietly affirmed, "That was an appropriate response." We connected for a moment and I believe that there was an instant of understanding that made a difference in his engagement in the lesson for the day, perhaps even his final output. If nothing else resulted, the moment itself was enough.

Due to the short-term nature of many writing residencies, teaching artists are in a business that requires garnering trust with students quickly. I ask students to buy into my plan, to drop hesitancy and fear, to rely upon me, and somehow I expect that most will. Then we get to work. In more than a decade of teaching work, I have discovered that during the first two days of a residency the students impose a variety of tests regarding trust and engagement, regardless of grade level. I must establish that I am the tour guide for a proposed journey; students are the travelers. By the third day of my residency, the lessons generally tend to flow better and students are more likely to commit their attention to the tasks at hand. They are also more inclined to contribute to class conversations. I am big on the conversations, particularly fond of questions and the resultant discussions. Teaching is not unlike improvisational street theater in many ways. Critical thinking starts with a series of provocations, inquiry that strays sometimes from the necessary routine of the classroom. Respect for the requirements and purpose of daily objectives must be counterbalanced with the unexpected. Students have an inherent intelligence and capacity that flourishes with arts-based learning, and poetry falls into that learning thread.

After teaching for a number of years, and particularly with my background as a workshop facilitator in a juvenile-detention center, I prefer to enter with limited preconceived notions regarding student abilities or limitations. In my juvenile-detention work, I discovered that if I learned the reasons for their incarceration, I treated students differently. When all of the young faces before me were just humans, rather than young people labeled "criminal," I was more open, and I had higher expectations of those individuals.

During a recent residency in an urban middle school in a depressed neighborhood with a 98 percent African-American student demographic, my partnering educator informed me that she believed I did not understand how to work with "these kids." Daily she suggested that I retool my approach to direct students toward the literacy skills she believed they lacked. Maybe a rapper was better suited to work with "these kids," she posited on my final visit. I was uncertain if she was referring simply to the 30 students with whom I worked that week, or was it a blanket statement about the entire student population.

Students demonstrate willingness and success in learning when provided stimulating, creative activities. In addition, if given an expectation of achieving at a higher level most people will attempt to reach that benchmark, if not overachieve in that direction. But if a low or no standard is established, they will reach that as well.

At the same moment I was told that I cannot expect "these kids" to produce, that "these kids don't have vocabulary" to create written responses to my prompts, I witnessed eager young writers with dictionaries and thesauri open on desks, heads bowed, pens and pencils making conscious changes in word choice. There was written language, thick with emotion, stretching the lengths of the pages before "these kids." Eight or 10 other students were riveted in front of monitors, typing their work with enthusiasm and pride. In fact, each of "these kids" produced an homage poem to someone in whom they had unshakable trust. They printed copies for me, for the teachers, a copy for themselves, and a copy to deliver to the person they honored in poetry. The poets read to each other and they fully achieved my expectation of the best effort they could muster to translate emotion into imagistic language that made them proud. The poems were often humorous and touching as evidenced in these samples from seventh-grade students.

She's a Goddess

She dances like the stars when it's time for bed.
She sings like a goddess on the first spring morning.
For a statuesque woman she is quiet as a mouse
but you can feel her presence.
When she's hungry she has a fit
instead of throwing a tantrum
she throws lightning.
Her eyes represent the sky they are emotional.
As she moves around she can't be still

the earth affects a tumbling earthquake.
I can't describe her face maybe you can she looks like Lora London.
When she touches you she leaves her mark.

—Malaysia

My Sister

My sister is very diminutive just like a lamp.
She is brilliant like a calculator.
My sister's hair is black as charcoal.
Her smile is very enchanting.
When she cooks it smells like the best restaurant.
When she goes out with her friends she guffaws like
Bigfoot.
She also researches cooking at school.
Her smile is gargantuan like a building.
She always teaches me responsibilities.
I also Teach her patience.

—Jaquan

This is a cautionary tale. There is something dangerous lurking behind the words "these kids," a term many of us have used at one time or another. There is an otherness. There is lack and limitation, fear and frustration. And there is division. "These kids" are often born of poverty. "These kids" are often children of color. "These kids" are presumed to be neglected and ignorant, with parents presumed to be abusive or absent. "These kids" may be differently abled. There is a lot under the surface of this language that becomes self-righteous and, if we buy into the premise, we perpetuate low expectations; we perpetuate the lie that "these kids" are somehow different, that lessons must be dumbed down because they will not be able even to focus, much less respond. My challenge in each residency: to engage students in ways that demonstrate that I do have expectations, and that I assume each of them has the acuity to fulfill them. I also do not assume students in a suburban classroom are necessarily any more skilled, willing, or happy than the young people in urban schools. I know better. Rural-school kids are not any more likely to be engaged with my proposals at first, nor are their home lives more idyllic than those of inner-city children.

Each time I leave a school, I leave behind a collection of poems that may provide teachers another lens for viewing their students' talents, capabilities, even personal circumstances. Unfortunately, I frequently do not even see the final product of our work because I am rarely in a school more than five days; therefore, the final revisions of the poems are often completed after I leave. My last day is a bit sad, but we celebrate our achievements in simple ways, mostly loud ovations and praise. Even the students most reluctant on days one and two ask why I need to go. Leaving is as much a part of the job as arriving, but bittersweet.

Students may access deep emotion as they work. On the last day of the residency I cited earlier, one student was grabbing every moment she could manage on the library computer to work on her poem, a raw yet beautiful piece more than three pages long. She arrived at school early that morning to capture her thoughts before first period. She spent her entire lunch period composing new stanzas. This student had a troubled history and she was finding safety on the screen as her words filled her view. At midday, she had an explosive outburst in another class, and it was likely she would not be permitted to attend my last session. I was disappointed. The same teacher who previously challenged my ability suggested that perhaps this behavior was the young lady's way of dealing with separation; this student was going to be abandoned, again, by another adult, and that adult was me. Perhaps she felt more empowered by creating the separation herself. I have encountered this sort of behavior before. In fact, it has been digging at me for several years, particularly when I work with youth who are classified "at risk." Am I fulfilling their distrust of adults by expecting respect and engagement, and then disappearing?

This abandonment issue is diminished in schools with which I have multi-year contracts. I may be there for only five days in an academic year, but students may see me in the halls the next year. Or I may even be in class with them again, which makes the whole process of connecting with students easier. I may have taught the middle-school students in the desks before me when they were in elementary school; or we may meet again a year or two later in the halls of the high school. This continuity of my presence, my becoming part of a school community, permits much less struggle. The trust tests I face are not as difficult because I am a known entity, at least to some of the young people before me. I may also be more of a known entity to the teachers with whom I collaborate and we become a more effective team. The teachers know what to expect and how to assist me in facilitating this particular learning.

I fear being another adult who walks away. I do my best to affirm these young people as valuable and bright; I believe in them and will remember them. Then I collect my hugs, sometimes sign autographs (an act that always cracks me up), and sign out of the visitor log to head home, sometimes just across town, sometimes hundreds of miles from the students I leave behind. But I leave them in full faith that they have witnessed their own competence with language; that they know how to communicate more creatively and effectively with others. If this is the case, then I have done my job well.

WILLING TESTOSTERONE

On Working with the Purpose of Life Ensemble

Quraysh Ali Lansana

Kuumba Lynx began promoting a ½ Pint Poetics Poetry Slam for young people between the ages of 8 and 14 in Spring 2009. Founded in 1996 by three dynamic young women, Kuumba Lynx is a Chicago arts-in-education organization employing Hip-Hop culture as both an art form and a vehicle for intergenerational and cross-cultural dialogue. The ½ Pint Poetics Poetry Slam is an ingenious program that fills a wide hole in the city's vibrant poetry community. Chicago is the birthplace of both the National Poetry Slam and Louder Than A Bomb (LTAB)—the nation's largest youth poetry festival. A natural outgrowth of these citadels of the spoken-word movement, ½ Pint provides an opportunity to engage youngsters who are not yet old enough to participate in the previously mentioned programs.

In response to the mesmerizing hold of Hip Hop/spoken word on my two oldest sons and their posse of highly motivated, soccer-loving friends, the Purpose of Life Poetry Ensemble (POL) evolved as a way for my family to address this interest and to participate in the ½ Pint Poetics competition. We then invited parents of other creatively-minded sons from our cultural community to help shape the ensemble. All of the POL boys have attended LTAB events and festivals, produced by Young Chicago Authors, for many years prior to the existence of ½ Pint. Most of the POL crew suffers, for better or worse, from culturally-aware parents who drag them hither and yon between soccer practice and video games. The boys were always invested in the LTAB competitions, as if they'd been watching World Cup matches or Ohio State football. You will see from my son Nile's essay to follow, they all like to win. It was refreshing to see a group of young Black boys, clearly friends and thinkers, amped up by the presentation of language and ideas.

I have never been a fan of or participant in the poetry-slam movement, though many close friends are stars in that community. The poetry slam was invented in the late 1980s as a way of making a poetry reading more engaging for an audience. This form of competitive performance poetry has become an international phenomenon and a spoken-word genre. The slam made a sport of poetry, often sacrificing prosody and craft for high scores and applause. Coming to grips with the competitive aspects of ½ Pint has not been easy. As regularly mentioned at slams far and wide, I acknowledge that poetry is the point. I cling to that notion and shared it openly while working with the ensemble members. However, when POL came in second in 2009 and third the following year, what they internalized was, "We lost again."

What drew me and the other parents to form, schedule, and maintain POL was the focus on social justice, in addition to creative expression. Despite distractions, hectic schedules, and an endless supply of energy, the boys focused when needed and worked very hard. Yes, they enjoy the spotlight and the potential for income from public performance, but I believe they also all like expressing their thoughts creatively while pursuing answers to questions about the world.

The first POL poem, penned in 2009, is titled "Melt the Guns." The poem was born of very real, very immediate concerns about gun violence in Chicago, particularly among young people. The city led the nation in the number of murders of high school students that year. The shooting of a young Brown or Black man seemed to appear daily on the local news outlets. I'm sure these killings were discussed in schools, even if informally. The sound of gunshots remains a regular occurrence near the homes of many POL ensemble members. We discussed the many reasons these shootings happened and what we might do to stop them. The poem closes with the boys chanting "Melt the guns, bring the peace!" then, at the vocalized sound of a gunshot, they all collapse to the floor. It is a haunting reminder of urban daily life.

Most of the POL boys are leaning into their teenage dispositions. What were formerly recreational activities are now serious commitments. Five of the boys are on traveling soccer teams that practice four times a week, and play multiple games on weekends. Nile and Troy are on a nationally competitive football team, and Onam's moves have landed him a spot in a citywide dance program and a photo in the *New York Times*. Girls have entered the picture, as well. I am unsure what the future holds for Purpose of Life. However, I believe these two years spent bonding, writing, and performing their own ideas have been valuable to all of the participants. Their level of comfort regarding public speaking has increased significantly. That is a given. Their capacity to access their thoughts, then consider and clearly articulate them, is a gift to themselves that will aid in their journey from boys to men.

The Purpose of Life Poetry Ensemble

Nile Lansana, age 13

Our group *Purpose of Life* (POL) consists of eight Black boys between the ages of 10 and 13, including three pairs of brothers, who love to win and who came together to write poetry and perform it for competitions and events. My experience with POL has been good. We have a lot of fun making, writing, and performing our poems. We started in Spring 2009.

We have mostly written about social justice. We researched different issues, such as the earthquake in Haiti, and violence in Chicago and around the world. For the poem "Haiti in 3-D," we looked at pictures from the Haitian earthquake, including a picture of a living boy trapped in the rubble of a crushed building. We wrote our thoughts and feelings about the pictures, the earthquake, and the devastation that was happening in Haiti. And then we formed it into a poem and started to memorize our parts and make the performance for the competition. And the final product was a poem that got all "10s" in the ½ Pint Poetics Competition, produced by Kuumba Lynx.

Haiti in 3-D

Destruction

Devastation
Desperation
 (Repeat 3X)

BOOM!!!

Rocks on my body
Dirt and cement all over me
Mouth full of dirt

Constant struggle against time
A child buried in gravel from the
tremble in Port-au-Prince

My skin is not black but gray
Got that aftertaste in this
nightmarish reality
I hear American words

Why are these people here?
Where are mama and daddy?
Why did this happen to me?

I do not want to die
Hold on
Just a little longer
I'll make it out
Survive any way possible

The stench of decaying bodies
And lost hope all around me
I am lucky
I am not dead

Haitian kids have lost it all in 3-D

A ratio of 7.0
Shook the Haitian capital
We need to help
Cause they're in need
They shouldn't have to plead

When Americans go to school
Sometimes we aren't grateful
When Haitians go to school

They are thankful
For the chance to learn
And the chance for life
And they thank God
It's not over with a knife.

It makes me angry no one cares
anymore.
They are still suffering

A bum out here is a Trump out
there
The poorest Chicagoan is filthy rich
in Haiti
Makes five dollars feel like five grand
Might make you feel like a man
While body after body rots in the
sand

The news stopped caring about
Haiti
But we will never stop.
Haiti has always been poor. They
never got help
I will be the one to help them.

I will be the one to help them no
matter what
I will give money to charities that are
helping Haiti
I will help build houses in Haiti

We wrote this poem to remember
and never forget!
We wrote this poem to remember

and never forget!
We wrote this poem to remember
and never forget!

The first Black Republic!
The first Black Republic!
The first Black Republic!

BOOM!!!

> —Purpose of Life (Devonte Ash,
> Josiah Ash, Troy Blakey, Ahmani
> Davis, Stokely Davis, Nile Lansana,
> Onam Lansana, Banu Newell, Evan
> Wimberly)

My favorite poem that we have written is "Purpose of Life." I like this poem because we got to be creative and think about different races and their lifestyles. The poem is also about the right way to live your life and how we are all connected to the earth and the innovators in the world and our lives.

Purpose of Life

Every life has a purpose
No man or woman can deny
You will find your purpose
Or you will die

Some people die for their purpose
That ends their lives in vain
So be successful and keep choo-chooing
Like an unstoppable train

Chilling out with no doubts
Starting no bouts
Making sure no one roars
Giving back to the poor

To make a difference in the world
Big or small, to help others
And fight for what is right
Don't give up on the purpose of life

Help is not a verb it's a noun!

There is a purpose in life
That you shall unlock
Find your key you must
Or live your life in shock

Some say life is nothing but strife
So they end it with a knife
Don't close the door on someone in pain
Helping them could lead you to fame

No, fame is just a lame game
That can cause you to stray
Away from the purpose of life
Which is helping the yelping
Not leaving the grieving
Saving the waiting in need of love
We can help them by praying to God above

The purpose of life is love!
I am
Connected to the earth

I am
Connected to people who care for the poor

I am
Connected to everyone I live for and with

I am
Connected to all African kids
Even from here on the South Side of Chi

I am
Part of a loving, giving, caring
Big, Black family
Where I live
On the South Side of Chi-town

I see
Overpopulation and poverty

I hear
Devastation same as in Haiti and around the world

We are all connected!

The purpose of life for me is
Providing, living and learning

They call me Chinese
When I'm Korean

I am teased every day
They say, "Ching Chi Cho"
They ask me to say, "wax on wax off."

Being Asian does not mean I know karate

Or work in a cleaning factory

I am Korean
I am American

Why can't I just be me?

The purpose of life for me is
Providing, learning and living

They call me Mexican
When I'm Venezuelan

Every day I am teased
Like I jumped the gate
Where's your green card?
That has not been used in 30 years

Being Latino does not mean I have the power
to jump over any fence
I can barely make a taco
I make no dollars, only cents

I only get the crummiest jobs
Harassed by cops for having an accent
I am an American, why am I threatened
Branded an illegal immigrant

Why can't I just be me?

The purpose of life for me is
Breaking the racial barrier

I have as much power as anyone
But we are forced into places

Categorized as the ghetto
African Americans are not
all gangsters and crackheads
We do not have a mysterious attraction
To KFC, Grape Kool-Aid or Cheetos

I am not stupid just because
I do not use words that are
used to oppress us

The purpose of life is
Unity
Hope
Keeping it real
Creativity
Passion
Determination
Dedication
Commitment

Purpose of Life!

—Purpose of Life (Devonte Ash,
Josiah Ash, Troy Blakey, Ahmani
Davis, Stokely Davis, Nile Lansana,
Onam Lansana, Banu Newell, Evan
Wimberly)

Even though we came in third place in 2010, our group's poetry won the award for the best social-justice content at the ½ Pint Poetics Competition. I personally think we should have won because I think that we had the best poetry and really good performances for both poems. And I don't think that some of the other groups had poetry as good as ours.

My favorite POL performance was at the Taste of Chicago, the big downtown outdoor festival that occurs every July. This is my favorite show because we messed up and we knew it. But we kept going and my brother Onam did a pretty nice improv and the audience loved us!

I want to be a soccer player when I grow up. I think POL helps with that because we have to have teamwork and commitment when we write our poems. You also have to be dedicated to the group. And you need all of those qualities when you play soccer as well.

I don't think most kids my age think or care about political issues. We hear about Haiti and we feel bad and sorry for them. Sometimes, we talk about it. But we don't really want to take action on the issues because we think it's just more work. With schoolwork and sports and friends and other things, adding "Save Haiti!" to our schedule just seems too overwhelming for us.

I think that writing about social justice has really opened my eyes to become more aware of violence and what's happening around the world. I think that it's a good thing to know what's happening around the world because you gain knowledge about what is happening and how it could affect your life.

"THE DIVAS" OF THE NINTH GRADE

Georgia A. Popoff

When we are young, so many of us are in a rush to grow up. The allure of adulthood is romanticized and the perception of freedom is compelling. This seems to be most evident with high-school freshmen. They get to the "big school," and the rush to independence takes on a new velocity. The boys morph into men, the girls suddenly possess a new awareness of their gender's attributes. And they become startlingly aware of each other. If middle-school teachers suffer from the challenges of teaching "hormones on foot," then high-school teachers are even more afflicted by the parade.

Male and female students issue their challenges to authority in different ways, but high school is the place where the conflict between not-yet-grown and the adult world appears most dramatic. I generally appreciate ninth-graders. They recognize the newness of their world of secondary education, they are often articulate and passionate about their feelings, and they may be open to receiving new insights regarding politics, social justice, philosophy, and learning. They are formulating opinions and their discussions are often very animated, generating healthy dialogue that may lead to more acceptance of others' thoughts, views, even personal identities.

During a recent school year, I entered a class with my usual enthusiasm. In the back row: a small group of young men isolated from the rest of the class, indifferent to the teacher and me. On the right side of the room: a row of young ladies engaged in conversation. Another cluster of young ladies broke rank from the rows of desks to create their own territory in the far-left corner. If Billy Crystal's *Saturday Night Live* character Fernando were to walk into the room, he would have gathered that these ladies lived by his motto, "It's better to look good than to feel good." They were checking their carefully coiffed hair, their lipstick, gabbing about important details.

Half of the class sat close to the front, creating a demilitarized zone for learning, bordered by disinterested peers. The teacher graciously introduced me. My first mistake of the week was in not recognizing the territorial boundaries in this classroom at that moment. There were ring leaders and factions of disenfranchised teens. Some were belligerent and unafraid of confrontation; they actually preferred it. The girls in the back were the most aggressive of the students in their flaunting disregard for manners, authority, and decorum, much less respect for the classroom. The class was an integrated environment. It just happened that this group of disruptive young women were Black or racially mixed. More significantly, they were a clique and they were, by their own repeated admission, party girls.

The gentlemen in the back were not confrontational, simply aloof and uncaring, for the most part. The exception was one young man who was less often in class than In-School Suspension (ISS)—an unproductive form of warehousing students, thus isolating them from the learning environment and their peers. Once he was removed from his crew, they caused no trouble, yet participated not a whit at first.

The young ladies were different. It only took until day two for me to lose patience. In my inner dialogue, I thought of them as "The Divas." I attempted to engage the class in reading poems by Langston Hughes and Nikki Giovanni in a layered approach, with repeated recitations and discussion. The Divas and the boys in the back stopped progress. I grew silent, trying unsuccessfully to wait out the side conversations. I attempted to draw the class into drafting first stages of memoir-based poems as a way of shifting focus and gaining buy-in. Still I met with resistance. Finally, I delivered a stern lecture on how the best way to receive respect is to offer it first.

People tend to approach one another with one of two attitudes. One temperament respects others until it is proven he can't; the second respects no one until it is proven she can. With all the talk on the street about who is "disrespecting" whom, the violence that I have seen arise over the smallest perceptions of rudeness frightens and offends me. In Syracuse alone, the upstate New York mid-sized city in which I live, several recent street slayings have been sparked by one young man believing that another was disrespecting him. In one of many cases, a 15-year-old with a handgun shot a man on the street in broad daylight simply because he did not like how the man was looking at him as they approached one another. We take such drastic steps to preserve respect on the street; meanwhile, members of this class disrespected the teacher, me, and their classmates. I felt obliged to articulate how much that offended me and attempted to advocate for those who really wanted to learn and participate.

The teacher actually thanked me in the department office later because she had been so frustrated with the class throughout the school year. She questioned her ability to reach the students. Trust me, it wasn't her. Although she was in her first year of teaching, this is a second career for this woman, and she is excellent and quite intuitive as to student needs. It was just her first rough crew.

The Divas continued to challenge, disrupt, stall, argue—with each other and with me—and primp. Three days out of four, I had to stop class to deal with these human roadblocks to the process. All the while, the island of learners sat up-front, gathering what they could between the intrusions. I lost my temper several times.

I brought out my standard discourse to classes that are so split and disturbed by reluctant learners. *Every time someone is rude and disrupts the class, every time your teacher has to stop instruction because someone is acting out, that person is stealing from you just as if he were putting his hands in your purse or your pocket and taking your cash.*

As flawed as our public-education system has always been and as deteriorated as it is today, it is still a privilege to go to school for free. Those of us who have visited countries without the economic advantages of the United States in the last 60 years witness the difference. Those who have immigrated from refugee camps or poverty-driven nations understand. Often young people do not consider how hard many of our elders and ancestors fought; they require reminders that many were beaten, jailed, even died in the process of securing a free education, an integrated classroom, a privilege for all citizens of our nation.

The lecture continues: *Why is that person stealing from you? Why is that my metaphor?* We discuss the options for young adults, the statistics equating earning potential with rate of education. *Now, the problem is that these people steal your time, your education. You are still responsible for passing the tests, and they take the time you would be learning right away from you*

175

day after day. The teachers cannot stop them. Only you can make it stop, by not accepting this behavior.

Every time I have to deliver the sermon, I present the idea and see how it goes. Sometimes I receive a positive response, at least for the moment. In this case, that was not the outcome. By day four I was at total odds with the Divas, and they got the best of me. They knew it. They did, however, write some. They were all bright but, as I said, they were party girls. And best friends. When they shared their work, the veiled references early in the week to the weekend parties, the alcohol and pot consumption, became bold, blatant by Thursday. It was obvious that during a recent vacation, this group of 14- and 15-year-olds had spent a weekend in the Bronx getting hammered and hailing cabs around the city from one party spot to another. I figured that they must have fake IDs and I am positive these beautiful, voluptuous young women looked like anything but the teenagers they are.

Every day I thanked each of the students who had invested their attention in class. I pointed out that this was their "home"—this class, this school—and the rude students were being disrespectful of me, their guest, of their peers, of their whole school. I objected to the behavior as a citizen, as an adult, as a human.

I don't think the die-hard obstinate students cared. There were "middle-of-the-road" students who were coming around, and then there were the ones I should have pulled aside to work with on our own, the group in front. In addition, while reflecting upon the particularly disruptive students, I question if elements of race, age, and gender were at work, affecting their attitudes. Both the teacher and I are White women; she is probably mid-30s; I am in my late 50s. It is possible that the Divas considered us irrelevant and dismissible because of our age and our lack of melanin. The Divas appeared to move through the world with solipsism and distrust of some adults, and perhaps I was one of them.

At the end of the fourth day, I was so disturbed I had lost my temper again that I went to the department chair to talk it out. I also apologized to the teacher, who replied that there was a permanent dent in the department office wall due to this class, so not to worry.

The plan was for Quraysh to join me on the fifth day, the last day of this residency. I had reservations about this period. Since some of the students in the class proved they had trouble containing themselves, they were two days behind the productivity of the other classes. I was uncertain they had earned the privilege of Quraysh's visit, but I considered my front row. I did request one thing from Quraysh if we decided to share that class. My preference is to be called *Ms. Popoff*, while Quraysh generally allows students to call him *Q*, since some people struggle with pronouncing his name. I said that the Divas needed that separation of status. If he wanted to allow the other classes to address him as Q, fine, but I preferred that he not allow that familiarity with this group.

Midweek I had announced that I was bringing my colleague, a college professor, with me and I honestly do not believe many students put the cue from Quraysh's name together with the possibility that Friday I would walk into class with a hip Black man with long dreadlocks. The Divas exchanged glances. Since I had also suggested to Quraysh that many of this group would not be able to conduct themselves maturely in the midst of his "Push-Button Words" lesson, I asked him to conduct an exercise in which he directs the class in a performance of Gwendolyn Brooks' "We Real Cool." The poem, without the title, totals 24 words that speak an entire scenario. "We Real Cool" presents a profound statement about the dangers of temptation for young people, particularly the temptations of disinterest, failure, and substance abuse. The poem is 50 years old and still pertinent, still chilling. When acted, it is powerful and draws students into the setting, whether they are "directing" from their seats or members of the "cast." The kinesthetic element and the amusement, coupled with the message, were perfect for this particular class. Ms. Brooks would have recognized each one of these young almost-but-not-quite adults.

Q has staged the poem countless times. Most of the roles this day were typecast, except for one of the Divas, one who could be distracted by her girls but who could also be drawn into the work at hand. She was chosen by the students sitting at their desks, the "directors," to be the leader of the crew. She embraced the role and took a firm stance of control.

In spite of the patient discussion Quraysh facilitated before the staging, word by word unfolding the bigger picture from the simple language, one Diva of the posse repeatedly forgot her three-word line. She finally gave up and returned to her seat, although Quraysh encouraged her to continue. It was just too much for her to remember. She was much more satisfied when she could command attention with her own rambling stories. An understudy took her place.

Several of the cast stepped up to the challenge and made the performance work. Another of the Divas kept whining that she did not understand the poem and demanded that Quraysh explain it to her. "What does it meeeeeaaaannn? You HAVE to TELL me." In spite of the lengthy discussion as the class interpreted the poem as a group, she held her position until the very end of the period. She didn't want to think for herself, she wanted to be told how to think, to be given the answers. It was not her responsibility, it was ours. She appeared to prefer to allow the world to slide by without engaging in anything beyond her immediate desires. She was a stunning young lady who seemed to live for the weekend. Neither she nor her friends were embarrassed to share tidbits of their rambles. They thought the tale of one of them puking out the cab window was hysterical. The fact that this small group of young women hopped Metro-North trains into New York City for weekend parties with "cousins" caused me to question if this was a reportable incident. Were these multiple cases of parental negligence or of clever high-school deceit? Whichever, these young women were very proud of their antics and expected a great deal of attention for them.

In spite of small moments of resistance, the blatant disregard and rude interruptions that I had endured all week were gone. We managed the class successfully and I, thankfully, was done with that group. The Divas rushed out to the hallway into a cluster of screeching, laughing girls, around whom boys revolved like planets. As they left, I thanked the students who had been respectful, and then I thanked the teacher, wishing her luck for the remainder of the school year. While Quraysh and I moved through the halls on our way to the next class, I said, "That was completely different!"

Q replied with a single word, "Really?"

"Yep. They were light years better behaved."

"Why do you think that is?" Quraysh asked.

I felt that the difference was twofold; he is male and he is Black. Who knows if I am correct, but still I voiced my supposition. He commented that he thought it was his hair, that his dreadlocks established a connection to youth culture that reflected Lil Wayne and other celebrities the students recognize. I suggested that to a 15-year-old, he may be ancient. I am among the corny, although I am joking a bit now and was doing so with him. Still, Quraysh is of the opinion that there was a connection that his hair and presence permitted.

Throughout the school year, this class had been close to impossible to focus and to guide in a learning process because of the actions of less than one-third. The rest of the class had long before resigned to the power play. The two of us have debated the reasons for such striking difference in behavior this one day. Was the material Q presented culturally more familiar? No, because they had also read Nikki Giovanni and Langston Hughes poems as short as Ms. Brooks'. Was Q's presence as a Black man in the school setting a rarity? Not in this instance.

I wondered if Quraysh reflected a father's authority, or were these young women attempting to garner attention and validation. What caused them not to push him beyond civil boundaries? These questions have no tangible answers, at least none that we have found.

One day earlier in the week as I was passing out paper for a writing exercise, I struck up a brief conversation with a young man who had been quietly absorbing the lessons and the absurdity. I thanked him for being a receptive member of the classroom. Then I asked him a question I pose to students who are interested in participating, but who get shut down. "How do you deal with this?" He said, as others have also responded, "You get used to it." How sad. Eager students are kowtowing to the few who do not care.

In spite of the challenges, there are students self-directing their success. The front row of the class was comprised of eager faces full of curiosity and a sense of adventure in the world of thought. They offered me lessons, especially the lesson of the power of perseverance. They were going to take what they could from school and try to stay well away from confrontation with those in class who broke down the order. They engaged to the fullness of their ability, given the challenges. They cared and were creative young people with goals in school, as well as for the future.

On Wednesday, during discussion, I polled the class about the music they were listening to; it was obvious from the earbuds hanging from so many of their ears that music was important to them. The names of favorite artists were issued in fervent call and response. One young gentleman wrote his answer on a sheet in his planner. I bent to read "Lady Gaga." I smiled and he smiled back. I did not read it aloud because I thought he was choosing to avoid ridicule from classmates for his musical taste. The next day the same young man was as vocal as he had been earlier in the week. In fact, he was one of the learning crew who would always bring a positive word to the lesson, often stopping the Divas from spinning out of control. I had not been aware that the day before had been the National Day of Silence. He was not speaking as his act of solidarity with the Lesbian/Gay/Bisexual/Transgender community, a voiceless civil disobedience. I was touched by and proud of his strength and courage.

The teen years represent the phase in which we design the staging of our adult identities. In the middle of their madness, teens are clinging to ways they are validated. For every Diva who appears to orbit a planet of self-involvement, there are young men and women who express compassion, intelligence, a thirst for knowledge, and for a place in the world. Perhaps the example of willingness of the engaged learner will drown out the discord, or encourage reluctant students to give voice to their own abilities.

WALKING THE DISTANCE OF YOUR VISION

Connection between Self and a 21st-Century World

Georgia A. Popoff & Quraysh Ali Lansana

> What we notice, we notice not because we
> were asked to, but because it was there in
> front of us—and it became apparent that it
> had more to do with us than anything that
> was specifically brought to our attention.
> —Richard Lewis, *When Thought is Young:*
> *Reflections on Teaching and the Poetry of the Child*

Cable news networks broadcast a woman arrested on the floor of Congress for protesting during the hearings on a petroleum conglomerate's gross negligence. After a brief, impassioned statement from the back of the room, this woman, a fourth-generation Gulf coast shrimper, pours a thick syrup over her head in an individual act of civil disobedience that decries the greater travesty of the possible destruction of all that she has ever known of life and livelihood. She is arrested.

This news item presents the opportunity to highlight political action as something meaningful and personal. This woman's story is one of utter despair at the loss of a way of life that stretches back into the early years of the prior century. This is apart from the deadening water, the sticky demise of the wetlands, the international impact of the mishandling of an ecological emergency. One woman's intimate act of outrage is a voice echoed for all of those who are silenced and believe themselves to be powerless. This woman's individual deed is a metaphor for our conviction, as educators and activists, that there is a very serious personal investment in observing, acknowledging, and claiming the right to respond to everything in the world in which we reside. This is the substance from which poems are wrought.

One recent spring, a ninth-grade teacher collaborated with Georgia for a week, five classes a day, 25 to 30 students in each period. The second-floor classroom overlooked the high school's baseball field, so the first five minutes of each class presented an opportunity for simple observation. Students were charged with the challenge of noticing something that they believed no one else would see, and being prepared to state their findings to their classmates. It was early May, so there would be daily changes in the boughs of the trees, the color of the sky, the cloud formations.

One day, first period, during that quiet time for careful observation, the baseball field was green and dewy. By mid-morning, the teacher and Georgia noticed that the outfield was dappled with yellow as dandelion buds loosened in sun. By the third class, late morning, the entire field was sequined bright yellow. The period after lunch started with students gazing out at a field once again completely green. Both Georgia and the teacher were startled by the transition. They recognized the power inherent in the moment; each minute can be determined through simple noticing. This day, the power of change rested in the simple task of a custodian slowly defining the perimeter of the baseball diamond on a ride-on mower, casually beheading the morning's blossoms.

This school has a significant population of students from Spanish-speaking nations, of whom many are children of undocumented workers. These young people may, in fact, have been born in the United States; still, they are acutely aware that their accents, the smells of their family meals, the sounds of the music that accompanies backyard gatherings, are significantly different than those of their neighbors. They are also keenly aware of jeopardy.

The last class shared their discoveries of the landscape on the other side of the pane, including the shapes of clouds, the deepening green bathing trees, rooftops that could be seen early in the week but that were no longer visible. One young man, dark haired and cocoa skinned, declared that he noticed the man seated on the mower was not Mexican. With that simple act of conscious observation, in that singular sentence, a dissertation on living within the fetters of racism, classism, and unfair assumptions was outlined. This young man, Mexican American himself, painted a powerful self-portrait that placed him among those who stand outside of the pop culture image of *American*.

We believe students benefit from learning that they are not islands unto themselves, a concept that may run contrary to their stages of emotional development. As educators, we are engaged in the act of developing thinking beings. We are in the business of guiding intellects through a process of critical and compassionate thinking. Encouraging students to apply conscious examination of their immediate surroundings will create opportunities to employ this power of observation. Through careful observation, students clarify and respond to the world around them. It is entirely possible that through this process, our students will develop a stronger relationship with the larger world beyond the boundaries of their own communities. However, the process of becoming global citizens begins within the immediate community as students develop a consciousness that travels beyond self into a global perspective, personal politics, and a moral construct.

Poems provide a way for young people to define and articulate their political and moral beliefs, and to address community, national, and international issues. It is possible to arrive at the substance of a poem by employing the skills of a journalist. As every big picture is described in total, the sums of its parts must be considered. In other words, you can't kill Moby Dick by biting his tail. The following essay illustrates methods of observation that instigate greater opportunities to develop metaphor by focusing on the details of community, interaction, and self.

VERSE JOURNALISM

Observing Today, Constructing Tomorrow

Quraysh Ali Lansana

If you wanted a poem, you only had to look
out of a window. There was material always
walking or running, fighting or screaming
or singing.

> —Gwendolyn
> Brooks, *Report from
> Part One*

Why is the juicy scandal with the pithy celebrity front-page news when
so many truly newsworthy events lack the same fanfare?

I was a journalism student in the 1980s, both in high school and as an undergraduate. Though *All the President's Men*, the 1974 book and 1976 film detailing the investigation of President Richard M. Nixon and the Watergate scandal, is what lit a fire in me regarding the sanctity of "the public trust," I did not become a newshound and political junkie until my days at the University of Oklahoma.

Of course in the 1980s, just as now and always, the world was exploding: the dismantling of Apartheid in South Africa, the dismantling of FCC regulations, Reaganomics, the fall of the Berlin Wall, and, as always, war. These are huge, complicated events, perhaps too much for an elementary- or secondary-school student to ascertain in one sitting, but it is critical that students be knowledgeable of current news. Young people benefit from awareness of the world around them, whether their block or Iraq. Yet society seems to privilege with its full attention the latest public meltdown of the artificially-flavored pop star or high-profile athlete.

Explorations into a more cogent understanding of the world outside must be consistent and digestible, as they offer students an awareness of their own power to change the world. Many of us are in such a rush to maintain the topical that we fail to absorb meaning. That topical theme can be as local as last night's school board election, as national as the mishandling of the victims of Hurricane Katrina, or as international as the number of dead soldiers in Iraq.

Pulitzer Prize winner Gwendolyn Brooks proposed we localize the news of the day one clipping at a time.

In *Report from Part One*, the first of her two-volume autobiography, Ms. Brooks named her construct "verse journalism," and defined it as "poet as fly on the wall...poet as all-seeing eye." As Ms. Brooks taught, poetry can function as a vehicle to access a more robust, more human investigation of news and events. With the benefit of poetic license, verse journalism provides poets the opportunity to explore a topic from the inside out. But unlike traditional journalism, this construct leaves room for emotion, creative imaginings, and nuanced opinion.

During the 1950s, in the peculiar heat of the Jim Crow Era and the infancy of the Civil Rights Movement, Ms. Brooks read everything in her South Side Chicago home—multiple newspapers, several magazines and, of course, books. During one of the most turbulent periods in US history, so many stories and ideas filled her head and pen, including the integration of Central High School in Little Rock, Arkansas. Ms. Brooks considered "The *Chicago Defender* Sends a Man to Little Rock" her archetypal verse-journalism poem.

The *Chicago Defender* Sends a Man to Little Rock
Fall, 1957

In Little Rock the people bear
Babes, and comb and part their hair
And watch the want ads, put repair
To roof and latch. While wheat toast burns
A woman waters multiferns.

Time upholds or overturns
The many, tight, and small concerns.

In Little Rock the people sing
Sunday hymns like anything,
Through Sunday pomp and polishing.

And after testament and tunes,
Some soften Sunday afternoons
With lemon tea and Lorna Doones.

I forecast
And I believe
Come Christmas Little Rock will cleave
To Christmas tree and trifle, weave,
From laugh and tinsel, texture fast.

In Little Rock is baseball; Barcarolle.
That hotness in July...the uniformed figures raw and
implacable
And not intellectual,
Batting the hotness or clawing the suffering dust.
The Open Air Concert, on the special twilight green . . .
When Beethoven is brutal or whispers to lady-like air.
Blanket-sitters are solemn, as Johann troubles to lean
To tell them what to mean . . .

There is love, too, in Little Rock. Soft women softly
Opening themselves in kindness,
Or, pitying one's blindness,
Awaiting one's pleasure
In azure
Glory with anguished rose at the root . . .
To wash away old semi-discomfitures.
They re-teach purple and unsullen blue.
The wispy soils go. And uncertain
Half-havings have they clarified to sures.

In Little Rock they know
Not answering the telephone is a way of rejecting life,
That it is our business to be bothered, is our business
To cherish bores or boredom, be polite
To lies and love and many-faceted fuzziness.

I scratch my head, massage the hate-I-had.
I blink across my prim and penciled pad.
The saga I was sent for is not down.
Because there is a puzzle in this town.
The biggest News I do not dare
Telegraph to the Editor's chair:
"They are like people everywhere."

The angry Editor would reply
In hundred harryings of Why.

And true, they are hurling spittle, rock,
Garbage and fruit in Little Rock.
And I saw coiling storm a-writhe
On bright madonnas. And a scythe
Of men harassing brownish girls.
(The bows and barrettes in the curls
And braids declined away from joy.)

I saw a bleeding brownish boy. . . .

The lariat lynch-wish I deplored.

The loveliest lynchee was our Lord.

Founded in 1905, the *Chicago Defender* was once the nation's most influential African-American newspaper and became the first Black daily newspaper in 1956. The *Defender*'s impact was so important nationally that it served as a clarion call for "The Great Migration" of southern African

Americans to northern cities like Chicago during the early 1900s. Imagine, as Ms. Brooks did, the paper assigning an educated, big-city reporter to a small southern city to cover the desegregation of a high school in 1957. He might have his own preconceived notions and biases about what he might find there, given the prevailing sentiments about race and class.

The reporter takes us on a stroll through a town riddled with stubbornness and intolerance, yet finds rich humanness in the small, simple details of living:

> And after testament and tunes,
> Some soften Sunday afternoons
> With lemon tea and Lorna Doones.

Indeed, those details not only create the world in which Ms. Brooks immerses the reader, they provide an intimacy with the elements within that world, a tone and sentiment through the vehicle of everyday living. Among her many notable quotes, Ms. Brooks was enmeshed in revealing "the extraordinary in the ordinary." The primary vehicle for this poem is not the reporter, but the details and the manner in which they are unveiled that capture us, which in turn makes the encounter palpable. What the reporter "sees" is whole, inclusive, and not solely the monsters. It would have been easy to focus on the negative aspects of this painful, historic moment, or on the heroism of those nine young students.

But, Ms. Brooks didn't actually travel to Little Rock to authenticate this poem. She accessed this world through the news media, her imagination and a serious belief in all things right and just. She read and clipped stories about the pending federally-mandated integration of Central High School, some likely printed in the *Defender*, among other entities. Then she examined the situation from varying points of view. Ms. Brooks became a Black Chicago reporter and editor, multiple White Little Rock residents, a brownish girl with barrettes, and a bleeding brownish boy at the poem's close. This is the power of art. Art should move us to think, not tell us what to think.

The potential to engage students in this mode of teaching and learning about current events is valuable from many standpoints and has cross-curricular applications. Certainly, history and basic research are important aspects of verse journalism, whether the news item concerns the bonuses of Wall Street executives or the release of *Iron Man 2*. Students will glean a surface understanding of the event from a press clipping, but must ask questions of the people and actions that comprise the story for the exercise to be effective.

The *who, what, when, where, why,* and *how* questions provide entrées. After those are distilled and recorded, empathy is the required next step. How would I feel if I were a Wall Street mogul with a huge check? What if I were a homeless person hearing about these checks? How does Robert Downey Jr. feel in that *Iron Man* costume?

Novelist John Edgar Wideman, putting a twist on an old idea, is quoted as saying "Instead of writing that which you know, write about that which you want to know."[1] The hunger behind the pursuit of this new information will compel students to think outside of their normal patterns. Verse journalism melds the literary forms of journalism and poetry to create an offspring distinct from both parents. There are at least four elements that distinguish verse journalism from traditional reporting:

- Poetic form allows the opportunity for students to create an intimate relationship with a news item, to personalize it;

- Working in verse permits students to concentrate on particular aspects of a news item that they find compelling;

- By incorporating poetic license, opinions and beliefs may be reflected alongside the chronicling of an event in order to make a personal statement; and

- The opinions must function within the world of the poem, the poetic environment created, rather than merely offering a platform for dogma.

The concentration of place, how place and geography inform identity, and individual world view help create elements of self. In the verse-

---

[1] From remarks at the 10th Annual Gwendolyn Brooks Black Writers Conference, October 2000.

journalism construct, students may explore local and world events, but what about their own blocks? Every neighborhood possesses sounds, smells, sights, and characters. Yet often we bustle down the block taking those elements for granted, oblivious to change all around us.

Under the influence and tutelage of Ms. Brooks, who mentored me for the last 12 years of her life, and working in Chicago public schools for a decade, I ascertained the benefit of utilizing poetry as a method of comprehending not only the larger world, but the smaller world as well.

Many of the students with whom I worked on Chicago's South and West Sides had not ventured outside of the five-mile radius surrounding home and school. One of these schools, where I spent eight years developing and implementing the teaching of history through literature, educated young people who could see the Willis Tower (formerly the Sears Tower) from the playground, but had never even been on its first floor, let alone the famous Skydeck. Economics is only partly to blame. These students either lacked or dismissed their ability to change their world, so they saw no reason to explore it. We, as educators and parents, are complicit in this attitude.

The "community-awareness" curriculum was born in this cauldron at a struggling elementary school on the near South Side and inspired my poem below, which provides a boilerplate for the exercise:

seventy-first & king drive

> night smells catfish crispness
> while sista girl works them curls
> s's lounge buzz and slam
> as brothas basehead
> brothas boomin
> basehead brothas boomin
> bass boomin
> boomin base
> blowin the plastic in the used-to-be back window
> a baby boppin in the backseat

jackie's restaurant is always open
well, in july, until 11:30 pm
urban queens with Newport lips
hardened softness serving biscuits of like texture
leo's flowers, a fading pastel
succumbs to evening's wings
chicken wings

wild irish the bouquet of the 'hood

With this poem as a model, students are asked to consider various aspects of their community with particular attention paid to sensory awareness. By identifying a local character, a place of comfort (or distress) outside the home, and/or a key landmark (particularly one that a student believes is overlooked or underappreciated), students are directed to view their neighborhoods with fresh focus. This approach allows for celebration and recognition of value and beauty in places that sometimes are perceived from the outside as having neither. This lens is equally effective in urban or rural environments, and may also bring vibrancy to suburban cul-de-sacs.

Once the poems are completed and shared in a classroom reading, consider contacting the people and businesses referenced to go on an actual sensory walk of the community. Time and safety permitting, make arrangements for students to read the poems relevant to each person or site they visit. Ask the community members about whom poems have been written to say a few words about the changes he or she has witnessed over the years. A reciprocity develops between writers and their subjects, along with great teaching and learning moments, due in large part to the fact that students become teachers or tour guides and engage the neighborhood directly and positively. I have appreciated student excitement as they led me, a familiar stranger, through the blocks they call home. Stories and anecdotes not shared in class burst through with great joy in the telling. Ideally, this will introduce or further entrench a sense of ownership, inter-generational respect, and civic engagement. The notion of "think globally, act locally" is initiated first by claiming the block.

Yes, difficulties may arise, as any off-campus activity involves much planning and logistical concerns. When my students and I embarked on our first walk, at that Near South Side Chicago school, we could only travel on the east side of Cottage Grove Avenue since the project buildings on the west side of the street were controlled by a rival gang. I hope your issues are less traumatic, and the lesson plan remains valuable without the physical walk. But I believe the walk to be a priceless component of the exercise.

If the school setting does not permit the walk, perhaps for reasons as I have stated in urban settings, or if the school is not located with proximity to the neighborhoods or streets where the students live, there are other options. One is to have students draw a map of the places that would have been visited, displaying their maps prior to the reading. This mapping requires no supplies other than those likely already available in the classroom.

Where digital technology is available, the maps can not only be projected for the class to reference as the individual poet reads his work, but they can also become a way to link to other classrooms, schools, and communities in a cultural and poetic exchange. Another option is to use digital cameras to capture images depicted in the poems. Through connecting the photography element to the written word, broader literacy may be achieved. Linkages to visual literacy— visual-arts elements such as depth of field, perspective, texture, and focus—may be created and then reflected back into the writing process to further develop the poetic image.

A third alternative is to invite key figures from the community into the school for a recitation and an exchange with the students who wrote about them. Consider the possibilities if the students invite the pizza delivery man, the bank manager, and the Walmart greeter who appear in student work to join in a conversation regarding the community in which they all live, hosted by the school and the student poets themselves. This is a delightful spin on the standard annual career day as well.

A fourth option is to use the school building in place of the neighborhood. There may be a tier of characters in the school community who are vital, yet perhaps nameless or enigmatic to students: custodians, hall monitors, and lunchroom workers, to name a few. There may be exotic locations that are ripe for harvesting: the science lab, the faculty lounge, the staircase that no longer goes anywhere since the last school building expansion. There are sounds, smells, mysteries to investigate in every school.

Both verse-journalism and community-awareness lesson plans demand a deep personal investment from students and teachers. Both begin with an investigation and validation of the students' own thoughts and environments. That kind of buy-in, as a foundation for learning, is crucial to the construction of critical thinkers and informed consumers. If we can motivate young people to ask daily at least one difficult question of or about the world, whether local or global, and then seek the answers, they will build a greater path to their own sunlight.

Comprehensive Lesson Plan

Push-Button Words

Quraysh Ali Lansana

Objective: To help students gain an understanding of words or ideas that they find offensive and build a level of empathy regarding the power of language as it affects others, while strengthening their English language arts competency.

Applicable Age/Grade Level: The target group for this exercise is high-school students, though a teacher might determine that it is appropriate for middle-school classes.

Anticipated Time: Adaptable, from a single 45-minute session through a five-day process.

Materials/Resources Needed: Writing materials (paper, pen/pencil), dictionary, thesaurus.

Process Overview:

The Push-Button Words lesson plan has the potential to provoke a variety of very serious emotions in students. The elements of openness and safety to speak must be present in the classroom when employing this lesson plan. Students must feel secure and respected by both teacher and peers to fully participate and benefit from this activity. This is an excellent exercise for after-school or out-of school-time programs in community and faith-based settings.

Preparation:

Prior to class, identify a mode of artistic expression that contains language, images, and/or ideas you find to be uncomfortable or provocative. This example could be a poem, song, news item, DVD/video, video game, or book excerpt. Additionally, find a second option from the media listed above that you believe your students will find unnerving. Try to discover this option in pop culture or current events that are likely to be familiar to students. Some examples may include, but are certainly not limited to:

- newspaper article about the march on Jena, Louisiana, in 2007, and the questions around racism underlying the event;

- cable news broadcasts of the personal struggles with substance abuse experienced by celebrities such as Lindsay Lohan or Charlie Sheen;

- the video game Grand Theft Auto;

- reality television shows such as *Jersey Shore, I Love New York*, or *The Real Housewives of Orange County* or *...Atlanta*; or

- the dark personal moments between Rhianna and Chris Brown, or Whitney Houston and Bobby Brown, which would eventually lead to domestic abuse appearing in tabloid magazines everywhere.

Initiating the Discussion:

- Engage students in a brief discussion to establish the guidelines for a safe and respectful dialogue for the duration of this activity. Employ students' input to determine appropriate responses to one another's comments as well as methods to indicate that comments from others are pushing boundaries of emotional discomfort (e.g., "ouch" when one student or the teacher might share something that feels uncomfortable to another).

- Share with the class the source material you find uncomfortable. Ask students for their opinions about why you might find this material inappropriate. Be prepared to present the reasons this content disturbs you, including past

195

experiences, cultural or political history, or deep personal convictions.

- Following this discussion, present the material you believe your students will find difficult. Frame presentation of the material in the idea that, as an adult, you feel this material is disrespectful to young people. In the event that students do not share your perception, ask them to state their reasons and further engage the debate/discussion.

Moving into the Writing Component:

To prepare for the creative-writing portion of the lesson, distribute or ask students to take out their designated journals, folders, or clean sheet of paper.

- Ask students to consider their own push-button words or phrases someone might say to them at the playground, bus stop, basketball court, or lunchroom that would get under their skin, make them fighting mad. Direct them to write down that word or phrase and, in no more than a paragraph, define why this language has such impact. Prompt students to think about all the possible personal, cultural, and/or historical issues that affect their reaction and rationale.

- Next, ask students to ponder, and then write an answer to these questions: *How do I diffuse the power of this material? How do I dismantle the atomic bomb of this word or phrase?* Allow students ample time for this part of the lesson. This may represent 15 minutes of class time and will generate material they can use to develop a first draft of a poem.

- Encourage students to include the settings and situations, real or imagined, where the push-button word or phrase is directed their way.

Modeling for Poetic Structure:

There is no prescribed form or contextual order for this lesson. However, as a model, here is one idea you might suggest students use in constructing their poems:

1. Setting or situation in which push-button word or phrase is shared.
2. The actual push-button word or phrase.
3. How that word or phrase makes you feel.
4. Why that word or phrase has such emotional impact.
5. How you diffuse or intend to diffuse its power.
6. How you rise above the sting and move forward.

Drafting the Poem:

Outline the following requirements for inclusion in the first draft:

- Poems should be a minimum of eight lines.

- No one-word lines.

- Use as few personal pronouns as possible. Avoid dependence on "I."

- Review key literary devices and other language-arts elements your class has studied (e.g., sensory details), and ask students to incorporate those in their poems.

Revising for Success:

Establish peer work groups of four students each. Ask students to take turns reading their drafts aloud to the group. Take a moment to clarify the difference between critique and criticism, the former being constructive comments that suggest possible improvements, the latter being solely negative.

- While one student reads a poem, the rest of the work group listens carefully. Ask each of the other group members to write down at least two questions they have for the poet regarding the ideas or structure presented in the poem being discussed, including literary/prosodic elements that they notice (e.g., effective and creative rhyme, alliteration, word choice, etc.). As they share these questions and comments in the group, the author will respond, also writing down ideas or suggestions that he or she feels will advance new ideas or improve the poem, based on the author's intention. It is important to remind students that they have choices in the critique and revision process and that they, the authors, make the final decisions as to what will serve the poem best.

- As students read aloud in their groups, suggest that they consider these readings a rehearsal for sharing their poems with the full class. Ask students to share suggestions for emphasis and even gestures in preparation for the final reading.

- Ask students to revise their poems, encouraging them to dig deeper into the emotional substance of their work. Remind students to examine all aspects and perspectives of the push-button word or phrase and its affect on them. Include all relevant details explored in their writing.

- Once the revisions have been completed, instruct students to exchange poems with their group members for silent reading. Make sure students are aware they can offer editing suggestions and ideas for additional language or content at this stage as well.

Finalizing the Draft:
Ask students to review the comments from classmates and make revisions they feel are appropriate. As a final step, they should edit their work to ensure correct spelling, grammar, and punctuation, and to be sure they are satisfied with the poem's content.

Publishing and Performance:
As a reminder, creating a safe space for the public reading of these poems is paramount to the success of the exercise. This may be furthered by reading your own push-button word response poem.

Many students will not feel secure reading such private information aloud. That is completely acceptable, as long as they've participated in both discussion and writing exercises. It is also fine to ask authors if they are willing to allow a peer or you, the teacher, to share the poem with the class. Often, a student will choose to read her work aloud at this point or in the future because the offer to read for her demonstrates a respect for privacy and sensitivity to personal material. It may provide all the encouragement the student needs. Sometimes the issue isn't a student's reluctance to share personal subject matter, but a lack of confidence that he has written a successful poem or has the skill to read aloud.

Expected Outcomes:

- Open discussion of language that establishes or violates a personal sense of self, or is otherwise demeaning or disruptive.

- Poems that openly and honestly address cultural, ethnic, and personal sensitivities.

- Increased empathy and acceptance among peers.

- Students may also conduct research for poems by noted writers that would seemingly fit this theme, furthering their knowledge of poetry and social justice issues. The historical context of such poems would broaden the overall impact of the subject matter and response.

COMPREHENSIVE LESSON PLAN

The Community-Awareness Writing Curriculum

Quraysh Ali Lansana

Objective: To claim a sense of ownership of the communities in which students live and to express their pride and value for the people, places, and features of their surroundings.

> **Applicable Age/Grade Level:** This lesson is adaptable to all age groups and grade levels, modified by skills and maturity.
>
> **Anticipated Time:** Adaptable, from a single 45-minute session through a five-day process.
>
> **Materials/Resources Needed:** Writing materials (paper, pen/pencil), dictionary, thesaurus.

Process Overview:
Although it was developed in an urban setting, the Community-Awareness Writing Curriculum can be adapted to work with students in rural and suburban schools. The lesson plan can provide a template for a single day of poetry writing, or be expanded to incorporate exploration of areas near the school, visual arts (e.g., drawings and photos of the locales students choose to write about), and learning about the history of the community and how its population and economy have changed over time.

Initiating the Discussion:
Share the poem "seventy-first & king drive" included in the essay "Verse Journalism: Observing Today, Constructing Tomorrow," or a similarly themed poem of your choosing, to provide a boilerplate for the exercise. After reading the poem aloud, guide students in a line-by-line discussion of

the poem. Ask them to identify the sensory elements at work in each line.

Moving into the Writing Component:

Next, direct students to write responses to the following questions about their community. (Tell students their favorite place may not include their home or the home of a relative or friend, and that their least favorite space may not be school.)

- What are three sounds you hear regularly?

- What are three scents you smell consistently?

- What is your favorite place in the community?

- What is your least favorite place in the community?

- Who is the local character—the person everyone knows, for better or for worse?

- What is the one thing you would like to change in your surroundings?

- What is the one element you would retain?

The responses to these questions should be in blueprint or list form, with the exception of the local character inquiry, which must include a one- or two-sentence explanation of why everyone knows this individual.

Drafting the Poem:

After the students have compiled their responses, return to the model poem shared earlier. This time, ask students to identify descriptive adjectives that will aid them in describing their own environments.

Next, engage students in a quick review of the following poetic devices:

- Alliteration

- Personification

- Onomatopoeia

- Oxymoron

- Metaphor

- Simile

Ask students to create at least one example of each device listed above for their poems. They may, for example, cull a sound from their blueprint and employ onomatopoeia to bring that sound to life. There is no line limit, but tell students that they must write at least 12 lines with no one-word lines.

Revising for Success:

During the revision process, in addition to the standard tightening and tweaking, ask students to ponder other significant aspects of the community they might have missed. Encourage students to think about sensory language, ideas, actions, and setting in making word choices. Peer-to-peer review and critique methods may be incorporated into this lesson.

Publishing and Performance:

Schedule an in-class community-awareness poetry reading, allowing time for sharing stories and memories associated with the places and people that populate these works. These stories offer fodder for other community poems and narrative writings.

After the in-class reading, consider contacting the people and businesses referenced to go on an actual sensory walk of the community. Time and safety permitting, make arrangements for students to read the poems relevant to that person or site. Ask the community member about whom a poem was written to say a few words about the changes he or she has witnessed over the years.

Expected Outcomes:

- To introduce or further entrench a sense of responsibility and ownership regarding students' environment.

- To encourage intergenerational respect and civic engagement.
- To share responses, pride, observations, and reflections upon the world in which we live through poetry.

POSTSCRIPT

▦

Lessons Learned

Georgia A. Popoff & Quraysh Ali Lansana

We are two writers who approach our work from vastly different directions to the center that this book has become. In four years, we have made a journey together to share a sampling of the countless stories, anecdotes, and experiences we have witnessed in our 30-plus collective years of teaching. Quraysh lives far from his homeland; Georgia lives in the neighborhood in which she grew up. We have both known rural America and urban; we are familiar with suburban as well. When we walk into schools, we are used to varied reactions. Sometimes there are hurdles to leap before crossing the trust line. Sometimes there is a single sentence that cuts through the thick air between a classroom of new faces and ourselves.

Our work as teaching artists entails crossing over boundaries of class, race, age, and culture. Just as Quraysh does not teach solely in urban schools, Georgia does not work solely in suburban settings. We both have experience in rural, suburban, and urban education and with all levels of socio-economic class. When we each started our practice, there were virtually no professional development opportunities available to us as writers who wanted to work in schools and community. We jumped right into the deep end with poems and passion as our water wings.

We share the practice of entering classrooms with respect for all whom we will encounter, teachers and students alike. This is the starting point of our bridge-building to meet the objective of teaching our platform for poetry. We continue to grow as artists and humans through these experiences. We both agree the moment we stop growing will signal the need to retire from the work.

For all of the wonders we have witnessed, we have also encountered a series of hurdles that provided many lessons. Neither of us resonates with the "cookie-cutter" assembly program or poetry-packet approach, although we understand the practices. It takes time to develop a unique writing process for and with students, a process that builds both skills and confidence. In designing study units that meet the needs of the school or individual classroom, there is rarely adequate, if any, planning time with our teacher partners.

Schools are busy places and we have learned to let go of a host of assumptions. Never assume the school or particular teacher knows you are coming. Contact the school in advance of your residency to confirm your schedule and contact person. Have the main office phone number accessible as you travel. Introduce yourself to other key staff in the building, particularly if you are there for more than a day. This includes the security guards or hall monitors, especially the ones at the sign-in desk, the secretaries, the custodians, the library/media specialists. Each of these people may become a key ally. Visit the library, survey the resources, review books on the shelves. Discover what the school may already have available to you to insure the success of your work.

Be prepared with multiple lesson plans to draw from in case everything changes. Test schedules, fire drills, snow days, unexpected assembly programs, substitute and student teachers in the classroom during our visits all require adaptability and improvisation. Always have at least one revision exercise to share during the residency period. Travel with extra supplies (writing materials, pens, pencils, erasers, sharpeners, writing paper, dictionaries, thesauri, glue sticks, scissors, anything to support your lesson). Teachers have limited supplies and generally spend a great deal of their own money to keep their shelves stocked. Like them, make your local dollar store a regular stop during the school year.

Time is always limited. The average residency is short enough. Teaching a single 45-minute session is likely to be an engaging encounter, but it will not provide the impact and possible learning experience that a writing residency of at least five days will provide. A longer residency of 10 or 20 days is a gift that allows intensive engagement with students and classroom teachers.

Planning is essential to the most effective writing residencies but at times is lost in the shuffle, particularly for independent teaching artists. Cultural organizations and established writers-in-the-schools programs expect to have planning meetings with school faculty and administrators to develop themes, goals, curriculum, scope and sequence, and assessment strategies on behalf of their writers. The established program director may already have determined elements of the curriculum design before selecting a writer to teach the program.

The independent teaching artist may request the critical element of planning time, but has far less leverage to make it a reality. Without the advantage of advance planning time, the self-employed writer working in a school faces a greater challenge not only in planning lessons, but also in making on-site adjustments to those lessons when needed. Additionally, time to discuss how the residency is progressing and assessing the results may be equally limited for the independent contractor.

Whether working independently or through an organization, pay attention to the learning environment, the teacher's realm, and the school culture itself. Never assume the teacher is an ally or collaborator in the process but never assume he is not. The current educational climate places a great deal of pressure on America's teachers. We must enter as assets to their work, not as burdens. We have tremendous respect for the work that teachers do daily. It is our hope that the host teacher is fully engaged in our process with their students, and that we are providing additional methods for their own pedagogy; however, we must be prepared for the possibility that a teacher will leave the room, or otherwise not participate in the lesson and that we must lead the class without the teacher's input. We also require the confidence in our plan to continue under any contingency.

Sometimes the cafeteria food is surprisingly good.

Neither of us wants to know too much about the students as they are perceived by teachers and administrators prior to our visit. We prefer to establish our own relationships with the classes we visit. We have individual practices that initiate our engagement with students. As an icebreaker, in part because his is so unusual, Quraysh leads students on the phonetic, cultural, and historical elements of his name. He then asks students about their own names. Georgia relies on a handshake with each student. Through a standard business handshake, while also personally exchanging introductions with the young people in class, she is able to confirm pronunciation, even spelling of names, and comment on a detail of each of the student's names in recognition of their individuality. When engaging in class conversation, we recommend that teaching artists remember to ask students their names and use them readily. Explain in advance that you might sometimes forget and that is not a personal slight. It may simply be due to the number of students you meet throughout the school year.

Young people have x-ray vision for insincerity. Be authentic, always. Bring who you are, your best self to the classroom. But also remember that you are larger than life; in a way, a celebrity visiting the school. As Georgia responds when asked, "I'm famous, just nobody knows it yet." Humor is a crucial tool. It is important to not to take yourself too seriously yet you must maintain professionalism.

Behaviors and expectations of children have changed since we were growing up. The barrage of images and sounds, and the influence of ever-advancing technology have placed different sorts of weights and impediments on imaginative thought than experienced by young people of decades past. Today's students are also faced with a host of social issues past generations did not experience to the same degree: street violence, a waning commitment to learning, lagging literacy skills, broken family structure, the influences of media and technology, growing up too fast, you name it.

Teachers and administrators have generally been welcoming, but their expectations have changed because education has changed. We must always be conscious of the pressure of the assessment-driven climate. We believe that it is wise to be versed in the learning standards of each state in which we work, as well as in national learning standards, to maximize our effectiveness and value.

The climate of competition for funding has tremendous impact. The federal No Child Left Behind and Race to the Top statutes have changed everything about funding, teaching practices, and assessment. There is an overwhelming onus on teachers to bear the brunt of the slippage in American education, exhibiting a pressure that is palpable. Seasoned teachers are leaving the field or retiring early. Attracting new teachers has proven to be difficult, according to many reports. The tension is evident in many of the faculty lounges we have visited throughout the nation. We empathize and strive to provide additional creativity, process, and humor in a valuable manner that bolsters the teachers' own passion for teaching.

The field of arts-based learning has flourished over the past 15 to 20 years, but it is now jeopardized by two factors: the current state of education and the challenges to the American economy that affect funding for the arts and for education. Additionally, the rift between the pedagogical factions of arts education and arts-integrated learning has created confusion for artists, schools, and funders. The requirements of grant sources and funders' parameters direct the way both teachers and artists design their practices. General arts in education may meet with resistance since fine-arts specialists may feel threatened in this time when arts programming is being cut in the interests of reducing budget deficits. Another roadblock we face is the failure to include the creative writing discipline in the arts curriculum and learning standards at both state and federal levels.

On the writers' side, there has been a proliferation in the number of masters of fine arts creative writing programs in the past decade. On one hand, this is wonderful because there are more literary artists with advanced skills, increasing the supply of writers to work in schools. The downside is a flood in the market for writers looking for work. Since the competition for faculty positions in academia is so keen, this directs a lot of young writers toward teaching artistry as a career path, or a steppingstone to a career in higher education. However, this circumstance creates the need for effective training for individuals who want to do this work. It also begs the question, is every poet or writer suited for the work?

One of the advantages for teaching writers in K-12 education is that the writing arts can directly address issues of literacy and reading comprehension, along with creative and self-expression. This may sustain our presence in schools when other artists are faced with a deficit of work. We deliver approaches and skills that are needed to strengthen literacy. Although the other arts do the same, their educational value may be perceived as more abstract or more challenging to assess by the school or educator who is pressed for time and money.

There are so many considerations in relation to the themes of this book and the work we do in community. We could go on for a long time. What we really hope to accomplish is to provide valuable support to teachers and writers who want to use poetry as a heftier tool for creative expression, meeting greater needs of core curricula, and addressing the pressing issues of social justice.

If we have provided avenues along which teachers and students might travel to reach the infinite possibilities of self and world via poetry, while arming said travelers with both practical applications and pedagogical conjecture, then we have been worthy guides.

ABOUT THE AUTHORS

GEORGIA A. POPOFF is a community poet, educator, spoken-word producer, and managing editor of the *Comstock Review*. A teaching poet in schools and community settings, Georgia is writer-in-residence to several school districts in New York State. She also provides professional development to schools and community-based organizations and has presented at numerous conferences both nationally and abroad. Georgia served as central New York program director for Partners for Arts Education and was a board member of the Association of Teaching Artists. Currently she is on the faculty of the Downtown Writer's Center, the Syracuse chapter of the YMCA's national Writers Voice program.

Georgia's work has appeared in literary journals, anthologies, and web publications. Her first collection is *Coaxing Nectar from Longing* (Hale Mary Press, 1997). Her second book, *The Doom Weaver*, was released in spring 2008 by Main Street Rag Publications. In addition to creative writing, she has published critical writing in the *Comstock Review*, New York Foundation for the Arts *Chalkboard*, and the *Teaching Artist Journal*. In the mid-90s, Georgia was active in the poetry-slam movement, competing in the National Poetry Slam in 1994 and 1995, and she has produced literary readings and spoken-word events for more than 15 years.

QURAYSH ALI LANSANA is author of five poetry books, including *They Shall Run: Harriet Tubman Poems* (Third Word Press, 2004), and a children's book, *The Big World* (Addison-Wesley, 1998); and editor of seven anthologies, including *African American Literature Reader* (Glencoe/McGraw-Hill, 2001). He is director of the Gwendolyn Brooks Center for Black Literature and Creative Writing at Chicago State University, where he is also associate professor of English/Creative Writing. He was formerly on the faculty of the Drama Division of The Juilliard School and was a reading/language arts editor for Scott-Foresman (Pearson Education), Glencoe/McGraw-Hill, and Holt, Rinehart & Winston. Quraysh was lead consultant/contributing poet for the Jamestown Reading

Navigator *Poetry Slam On-line Program* and currently serves as a contributing editor for the *Writer's Chronicle* of the Association of Writers and Writing Programs.

He is the recipient of many awards, including the 2010 Alumni Award in the Arts from Chicago State University; the 1999 Henry Blakely Award, presented by Gwendolyn Brooks; and the 1999 Wallace W. Douglas Distinguished Service Award, presented by Young Chicago Authors Inc. A widely published poet, Quraysh earned a masters of fine arts degree from the Creative Writing Program at New York University, where he was a departmental fellow. A literary teaching artist and curriculum developer for two decades, Quraysh has led workshops in prisons, K-12 classrooms, and universities in more than 30 states, and was the inaugural professional development presenter for Chicago Arts Partnerships in Education.

ABOUT THE ARTIST

JOYCE OWENS is a painter works in two and three dimensions. She is the curator and professor of drawing and painting at Chicago State University. In college, Owens was the art editor of the Howard University literary magazine for three years, and was given her first illustration assignment by Random House. While earning her MFA at Yale University, she won the Helen Winternitz Award in Painting, contributed to the university's art and literary magazine, and created a poster for the historic Whiffenpoofs singing group. Owens has served as juror, panelist, consultant, or lecturer at the School of the Art Institute of Chicago, College Art Association, Illinois Arts Council, Arts Alliance Illinois, Chicago Artists Coalition, Chicago Department of Cultural Affairs, Columbia College, and Hyde Park Arts Center.

Owens' work has been exhibited at NATO Headquarters in Brussels, University of Pennsylvania Museum, Philadelphia Museum of Art, The DuSable Museum of African American History, Koehnline Museum, The Spertus Museum and Museum of Greater Lafayette, Indiana. She has own "best of show" honors in several national and international juried exhibitions. Other accolades include a 3Arts fellowship and Chicago Women's Caucus for Art award and the African American Arts Alliance award for Owens' achievements in the visual arts.

WORKS CITED

OUR HUMANIFESTO: A PROLOGUE, A POSITION STATEMENT, A PAIR OF POETS TALKIN'

Cixous, Hélène. *The Hélène Cixous Reader.* New York City: Routledge, 1994.

THE POWER OF LANGUAGE: THE STRUGGLE CONTINUES

Crews, Rudy. *Only Connect: The Way to Save Our Schools.* New York Farrar, Straus and Giroux, 2007.

Ingerman, Sandra. *Soul Retrieval: Mending the Fragmented Self through Shamanistic Practices.* New York: HarperOne, 2006.

DEMYSTIFYING THE POEM

Lewis, Richard. *When Thought is Young: Reflections on Teaching and the Poetry of the Child.* Moorhead, Minnesota: New Rivers Press, 1996.

Hugo, Richard. *The Triggering Town: Lectures and Essays on Poetry and Writing.* New York: W.W. Norton & Company, 2010.

ONE BAG EMPTY

Turco, Lewis. *Poetry: An Introduction through Writing.* Reston, Virgina: Reston Publishing Co., 1973.

STRETCHING EXERCISES

Lansana, Quraysh Ali. *southside rain.* Chicago: Third World Press, 2000.

JESTERS, AVATARS, AND LAYERED LANGUAGE: POEMS AS VIDEO GAMES

Tovani, Cris. *I Read It, but I Don't Get It: Comprehension Strategies for Adolescent Readers*. York, Maine: Stenhouse Publishers, 2000.

RECIPE FOR A SIMPLE START: POEM OF THE WEEK

Lewis, Richard. *Miracles: Poems by Children of the English-Speaking World*. New York: Simon & Schuster, 1984.

VOICING THE MARGINS

Jess, Tyehimba. *leadbelly: poems*. Seattle: Wave Books, 2005.

Cook, William A. "The Literature of Black America—The Noise of Reading," *Tapping Potential: English and Language Arts for the Black Learner*. Urbana, Illinois: National Council of Teachers of English, 1985.

GRASPING FOR IMAGINATION IN THE FACE OF FEAR

Lewis, Richard. *When Thought is Young: Reflections on Teaching and the Poetry of the Child*. Moorhead, Minnesota: New Rivers Press, 1996.

Gardner, Howard. *Frames of Mind: The Theory of Multiple Intelligences*. New York: Basic Books, 1993.

HAVE CAMERA, WILL TRAVEL

Smith, Charles R. Jr. *I Am America*. New York: Cartwheel, 2003.

POETRY AND DIVERSITY: LANGUAGE, EMOTION, AND SHARED EXPERIENCE

Carruth, Hayden. "Poets without Prophecy," *Selected Essays and Reviews*. Port Townsend, Washington: 1996.

NAME CALLING: THE LANGUAGE OF THE STREETS

Carter, D., Harrison, D., and Wilson, R. "Mrs. Officer," *Tha Carter III*. Cash Money Records: 2008.

THE SOFT BIGOTRY OF DIMINISHED EXPECTATIONS

Lewis, Richard. *Taking Flight, Standing Still: Teaching Toward Poetic and Imaginative Understanding*. New York: Touchstone Center Publications, 2010.

WALKING THE DISTANCE OF YOUR VISION: CONNECTION BETWEEN SELF AND A 21ST-CENTURY WORLD

Lewis, Richard. *When Thought is Young: Reflections on Teaching and the Poetry of the Child*. Moorhead, Minnesota: New Rivers Press, 1996.

VERSE JOURNALISM: OBSERVING TODAY, CONSTRUCTING TOMORROW

Brooks, Gwendolyn. *Report from Part One*. Detroit: Broadside Press, 1972.

Additional lesson plans and other resources related to *Our Difficult Sunlight: Poetry, Literacy, & Social Justice in Classroom & Community* are available on the T&W website: www.twc.org/sunlight.

Structure & Surprise: Engaging Poetic Forms, edited by Michael Theune. *Structure & Surprise* offers a road map for analyzing poetry through examination of poems' structures, rather than their forms or genres. The concept encourages using structure as a tool to see the fundamental affinities between different kinds of poetry and literary eras.

Handbook of Poetic Forms, edited by Ron Padgett. This bestselling handbook includes 76 entries that succinctly define the forms, summarize their histories, quote good examples (both ancient and modern), and offer professional tricks of the trade.

Poetry Everywhere: Teaching Poetry Writing in School and in the Community by Jack Collum and Sheryl Noethe. *Poetry Everywhere* contains 65 surefire exercises, more than 400 example poems, and innumerable writing tips and reflections on teaching the craft.

The T&W Guide to William Carlos Williams, edited by Gary Lenhart. Seventeen innovative essays by Julia Alvarez, Allen Ginsberg, Kenneth Koch, and others explore imaginative ways of using the work of Williams in the writing classroom.

Luna, Luna: Creative Writing Ideas from Spanish, Latin American, and Latino Literature, edited by Julio Marzán. In these 21 lively essays, Julia Alvarez, Martín Espada, Naomi Shihab Nye, and others share their experiences teaching literature from both Spain and the Americas. They discuss the work of Sandra Cisneros, Federico García Lorca, Pablo Neruda, and others.

Sing the Sun Up: Creative Writing Ideas from African American Literature, edited by Lorenzo Thomas. Twenty writers present original methods for inspiring students to write through readings of James Baldwin, Gwendolyn Brooks, Rita Dove, Zora Neale Hurston, and Jean Toomer.

Classics in the Classroom: Using Great Literature to Teach Writing, edited by Christopher Edgar and Ron Padgett. The unusual range of literature discussed in *Classics in the Classroom* includes Homer, Sappho, Rumi, Shakespeare, Basho, Charlotte Brontë, and Twain.

The Circuit Writer: Writing with Schools and Communities by Margot Fortunato Galt. *The Circuit Writer*, Galt's account of 30 years as a visiting writer teaching in the Upper Midwest, offers a range of exercises for use in creative writing classes.

Teachers & Writers Collaborative books are available from Amazon.com and other retailers.